The Book of
BURNETT

The Book of
BURNETT

42 Truths for Living Life Well, Fully, and Without Regret

NETTA FEI

VIDE INC

Cover design by Gerard Munajj | Graphic Image Design

ISBN 979-8-9901381-2-4 (hardcover)
ISBN 979-8-9901381-3-1 (paperback)
ISBN 979-8-9901381-4-8 (ebook)

www.nettafei.com

For Nundy's children and for Shiloh,
whose hearts also carry these words and
know that wisdom and truth stand forever.

Contents

The Book of
BURNETT

Foreword One

As the proud firstborn child of Burnett and Zelda Jackson, I had the rare blessing of spending long hours at my father's knee, learning the do's and don'ts of life. What he knew, he taught me and later my siblings. What he learned, he passed on to us. Not just through his words, but through the way he lived. Those lessons formed the quiet foundation of my faith and character.

Dad's truths wove their way through each moment of my growth—everything from riding a bike, learning the Bible, laughing at the carnival, doing outdoor chores, playing ball, and tying my first tie, to accepting salvation through Jesus Christ, driving a car, understanding relationships, and maturing into adulthood as a husband and father, starting my own family.

Later, when I answered my own call into ministry and had the privilege of serving alongside Dad as his assistant pastor for some fifteen years, I sat at that same knee again—this time learning the deeper rhythms of shepherding souls, knowing people, using "good" wisdom, and leading with both strength and compassion. Those lessons were priceless. They continue to steady and strengthen me today as I now serve as pastor of Shiloh Baptist Church, the congregation Dad led for nearly five decades.

As much as Dad's teachings guided our family and the lives of countless others toward success, sharing those truths brought him immense joy. He truly loved people and took great delight in lifting them higher. He believed that every conversation, every encounter, and every moment offered an opportunity to plant seeds of truth, encouragement, and faith. Even in moments of correction, his words were meant to build, not break. That kind of wisdom cannot be learned from books alone; it must be witnessed, absorbed, and practiced, and I was blessed to do just that.

Rarely a week passes that I don't speak with my brother or sister. Our conversations are filled with laughter, life updates, and—without fail—at least one truth passed down to us from our father. His voice still echoes in our lives, reminding us of the importance of integrity, kindness, patience, and faith.

Now, through my sister's tender work to capture these truths on paper, you are invited to sit at Dad's knee too—if only indirectly—and receive the same gems that shaped us. These words carry the power to sculpt your life too if you will let them.

That is my sincere prayer: that every page of this book will do for you what it has done—and continues to do—for me: serve as a faithful guardrail, keeping your steps in the godly way you should go, so that your harvests may be good and plentiful and harmoniously in flow with God.

Rev. Terry A. Jackson
Pastor, Shiloh Baptist Church
First son and child of Burnett and Zelda Jackson

Foreword Two

Heroes—real heroes—have a way of shaping you for life.

My father, Rev. Burnett S. Jackson, became my hero when I was very young. Not the flashy, made-for-movies kind of hero, but the rare kind who actually walks the talk and wears the hero suit with quiet dignity.

I knew him to be an excellent provider for our family. We always had food on the table, clothes on our backs, and a roof over our heads. He was an involved parent—present at school activities, Little League games, and everyday moments that mattered.

He was a God-fearing spiritual teacher, a steady church leader, and a pillar in our community.

More than anything, he was consistent. The same man in the pulpit was the man at home. The same faith he preached, he practiced. The same standards he taught, he lived.

Dad's way of being inspired me to be the same. His truths walked beside me in every season of my life: when I became a Christian; when I learned to trust God for myself; when I landed a good job that carried me to an unfamiliar city; when I met my soulmate and married; when we began raising our family; when I served in church and community; when I stepped into entrepreneurship; and when I built a brick home of my own.

Through every transition, Dad's voice never left me. His lessons followed me. His example steadied me. Even when I was far from home, I was never far from his wisdom.

On my standing Sunday evening calls with him and my mother, Zelda, it was there: questions, counsel, correction, encouragement, laughter, and the firm wisdom of a father who never stopped guiding his son.

As I raised my three sons, I did my best to live before them the same values Dad lived before me—faith, integrity, discipline, compassion, and unshakable trust in God. I wanted them to know his wisdom not only by what I said, but by how I stood.

Dad's words traveled miles and decades, but they always arrived right on time. His voice supported me in difficult times and reminded me who I was when the world tried to rename me. Even across time zones, he never stopped being my father and my model for manhood.

In this, *The Book of BURNETT*, the wisdom that I first began to hear as a child at our kitchen table and that then traveled to me by telephone now reaches you by page. These are not just sayings. They are lived lessons, proven over a lifetime. They molded our family, directed our choices, and continue to steer us still.

These truths anchor the reasons Dad remains my hero— unbroken in love and faithful in action, no matter the circumstance. He would often say, "Have faith in God, because if you make one step, God will make two." That one alone is a bonus truth worthy of standing beside these forty-two.

My hopeful prayer is that as you read this book, you will not only hear my father's words but you will feel his heart.

May these truths strengthen your walk, steady your steps, and help you live well, fully, and without regret.

Alfred Burnett Jackson
Second son and child of Burnett and Zelda Jackson

Preface

There was a man sent from God whose name was Burnett.

A man's man. An honorable husband for sixty-two years. A devoted father of three, grandfather of eight, and great-grandfather of three. A praiseworthy patriarch, loving and supporting family. A visionary who built the first brick home on a long rural road of wood-framed and block houses, opened a laundromat in the inner city, and led the construction of two brick churches.

A passionate Black Baptist preacher and pastor of the Calvary Baptist Church in Madison, Georgia for sixteen years and the Shiloh Baptist Church in Athens,

Georgia for forty-eight years. An attentive mentor, moderating an association of churches for twenty-seven years. A diligent anchor, serving fifteen years as the assistant recording secretary of the General Missionary Baptist Convention of Georgia and actively supporting its Baptist Training Union Congress.

And now, an ancestor rooted deep in the soil of our family tree—no doubt still preaching, still leading, still serving—dressed in a celestial three-piece suit with a cuffed shirt, gem-studded cuff links, matching tie and handkerchief, and a gold pocket-watch with its chain looped through the vest just so.

That man was my father, the Rev. Burnett S. Jackson.

Wherever there was an open seat and a willing ear—at the kitchen table, in the pulpit, on the front porch, or along the roadside—Daddy would slide wisdom across the table like a slice of sweet potato pie. His lessons were never forced. They were offered. Often simply stated. Always seasoned with life. And somehow, they landed exactly where they were needed.

With remembrances from my two older brothers, Terry and Al, I gathered forty-two of Daddy's most repeated truths and wrote them here as plainly and faithfully as I know how—carefully channeling and dictating what and how he explained it to me now. These are not lofty theories. They are weathered words—wisdom he bore or borrowed through experience, suffering, service, faith, and love.

Daddy did not just believe and preach these truths. He and our mother, Zelda, practiced them before us and before the tens of thousands of people who passed through their lives. And these guideposts produced for them good fruit. In joy and in grief. In abundance and in scarcity. In public and in private. And that is what gave his words their weight.

About a year before his death in December of 2020—just shy of his ninetieth birthday—he said something to me that still rings in my spirit. "I've lived a good life," he declared, brimming with confidence and deep peace. "I have no regret, and I'm ready to go."

That was not bravado. That was the quiet testimony of a man who had poured himself out fully.

This book is my offering to the world of the wisdom that shaped me, steadied my brothers, anchored our family, and uplifted countless others.

These pages hold my father's voice, his convictions, his laughter, his firmness, his compassion, his joy, and his way of living well.

As you read *The Book of BURNETT*, I pray that you will not only hear his words but that you will feel both their importance and their warmth. And that somehow, through these truths, you too might find yourself walking through life with greater clarity, stability, faith, joy, and yes—without regret.

Netta Fei
Also known as Burnetta Faye Jackson
Daughter and third child of Burnett and Zelda Jackson

Chapter 1

Talk is cheap. At the end of the day, what do you do?

1 When I would meet with inmates in our local prison, I often marveled at the remorse in their words. Many of them spoke of repentance and turnarounds and returning to church once they got out. I rarely heard from any of them again. The same with many people I prayed for in hospitals or counseled on domestic troubles.

2 Folks talk of this and that, of lies and truths, of visions and vows to be, do, live, and love better.

3 This is especially loudest when the proclaimer is the midst of trouble and in want of salvation.

4 I call it all "prison talk", promising any sweet thing in the hope of rescue.

5 There is a likeness between such talk and old pennies—both are easy to find, easy to spend, and low in value and weight.

6 In other words, talk is cheap and easy. It doesn't build shelters, mend fences, nor put food on the table. And anyone can possess it at any time.

7 It costs nothing to promise, nothing to declare, nothing to announce. Words flow freely when the stakes are low and the crowd is friendly. But when the lights dim, the applause fades, and life calls your bluff, only one question remains: What do you do?

8 I lived long enough to know that life does not reward good intentions. We all know what road is paved with those.

9 Life responds to action. It's the walk that matters. It's the doing that testifies. It's the fruit that bears witness to the seed in any situation.

10 Character is not proved by what a person says under bright lights. Character is revealed by what a person does in the quiet shadows of ordinary days.

11 Dreams without discipline are just bedtime stories. Faith without works or movement is only noise in the air.

12 You can talk about love all day, but how do you treat people when they frustrate you?

13 You can talk about integrity all you want, but what choice do you make when no one is watching?

14 You can talk about prayer, purpose, and promise, but what do your feet do after the "Amen"?

15 Some people speak in thunder and live in whispers. Others speak softly but leave footprints that cannot be erased. The world is full of good talkers. It is starving for faithful doers.

16 At the end of the day, children remember how you showed up. Communities remember whether you stayed.

17 God measures not just what you profess, but what you practice. Even your own soul keeps account. It knows whether you lived brave or hid behind beautiful words.

18 Talk may open the door, but only action walks you through it. Talk may spark the fire, but only action keeps it burning. Talk may plant the seed, but only action tends the ground.

19 So talk all you want. Speak your vision. Declare your faith. Share your hopes. But when the night settles and the day is tallied, let your hands agree with your mouth.

20 Let your steps confirm your prayers.

21 Let your life make the argument your words could not finish.

22 Because when the talk is over and the dust settles, what you've done will be your only true testimony.

23 At the end of the day, what do you do?

Chapter 2

Let your word be your bond.

1 Sometimes, a situation can land you in a place where all you have is your word to work for you, to act as a guarantor, to plead your case, to secure your release.

2 When that need arises, how good will your word be? How well will it work for you?

3 Will your word be regarded as ironclad as a signed contract or a recorded deed; steady as gravity and just as dependable as the rising sun? Or will it quietly betray you, calling you crooked and unreliable before you ever open your mouth?

4 Long before people measure your skills, your education, or your success, they measure your word—and they decide whether to trust you by how faithfully you keep it.

5 An old farmer living near our community agreed to sell another man a small piece of land with nothing but a handshake. No papers. No lawyers. Just two men standing on dirt and trust. Months later, when the property's value doubled and others tried to outbid the deal, that farmer never wavered. "A promise is a promise," he said, and kept his word at a loss to himself but a blessing to another. That kind of integrity outlives profit.

6 If the truth were told—and I'm about to tell it—your word is not small. It follows you into courtrooms, boardrooms, and back rooms, into friendships and into faith. It means something.

7 People may forget what you promised, but they never forget whether you kept it or not.

8 A person without a reliable word may speak loudly but stands weak. A person with a strong word may speak softly yet stands tall.

9 When your yes means yes and your no means no, trust grows fast and travels far. More than mere declaration, a consistent and proven pattern of actions

built with reliability over time, layer by layer is what creates integrity.

10 And when you honor your word, you mirror God's nature in small, human ways. Your words align with your true intentions and values.

11 You *say* what you mean and mean what you say.

12 You solidly *do* what you say you will do, fulfilling pledges and commitments, big or small.

13 You take ownership of your statements. If unforeseen circumstances prevent you from keeping your word, you clearly communicate so, take responsibility, and seek to make things right if possible.

14 You make agreements with consideration of your capacity to deliver *before* committing your word. Each kept promise reinforces the bond, while each broken one weakens it.

15 You speak truthfully, avoiding exaggeration or misleading statements that could damage future trust.

16 Basically, you become someone others can lean on without slipping.

17 So speak carefully. Promise sparingly. And when you give your word, guard it like treasure because once

trust is broken, it costs more to rebuild than it ever did to keep.

18 This is how to let your word be your bond.

Chapter 3

Haste makes waste.

1 I've known folk who like to do everything fast. They swallow their food in big gulps instead of tasting it. They drive the road like they're late for tomorrow. They "break their necks" to be first in line. They skim over details, skip instructions, rush conversations, and hurry through decisions—just to say they got it done. Speed becomes their badge of honor.

2 But have you noticed what happens when people live in a hurry?

3 Mistakes multiply. Paint spills. Glass shatters. Tools break. Furniture gets misassembled. Stop signs get rolled through. Words get released that should have been kept behind the teeth. Time gets blown. And sometimes, lives are lost.

4 And these are just a few of the visible wastes of haste—the ones you can sweep up with a broom or tally on a repair bill.

5 Yet there are also wastes you cannot so easily measure. Wasted chances to build emotional depth with a spouse or a child. The quiet erosion of meaningful experiences. The loss of understanding that comes only through patience. The missed satisfaction of work done with care and excellence. The forfeiting of wisdom that only shows itself to those who slow down long enough to notice.

6 All of it sacrificed at the altar of haste.

7 When you rush, you skim the surface of life.

8 You touch everything, but nothing touches you deeply.

9 Conversations become transactions. Learning becomes mere data collection. Creativity gives way to predictable output. Even worship of God can become routine when it is rushed. You arrive, perform, and depart—but never fully enter.

10 And the loss is not just in the task at hand. It is in your connection to the work, to the people around you, and to the present moment God is offering you right now.

11 Haste breeds a peculiar poverty—an abundance of motion masking a scarcity of attention, reverence, and engagement.

12 In your rush to *do*, you carelessly sacrifice your *being*.

13 Are you that one? Always in a hurry? Eating the sour fruit of hastiness while wondering why life feels thin and strained? Moving fast but feeling behind? Busy but unfulfilled?

14 Wisdom does not celebrate haste. It honors patience, diligence, and steady faithfulness.

15 The farmer does not rush the harvest. The builder does not hurry the foundation.

16 Bible tells us that even God, who could do all things in an instant, chose six days to create—and a day to rest. That alone says something sacred about the pace of purpose.

17 Haste often grows out of fear—fear of falling behind, fear of missing out, fear of not being enough.

18 But speed does not cure fear; it only masks it.

19 What heals fear is trust in God's timing, trust in sturdy effort, trust that what is meant for you will not pass you by because you moved with wisdom instead of frenzy.

20 Slowness is not laziness. It is intentionality. It is choosing accuracy and substance over speed. It is taking the time to read the instructions before turning the wrench. It is listening long enough to truly understand. It is pausing and praying before acting.

21 Yes, some moments require urgency. A rushed prayer is not the same as an insincere one. A quick decision is not necessarily unwise.

22 Still, urgency needs wisdom as its companion. Speed without discernment is just motion without meaning.

23 So slow down. Take time to think. Make calculated decisions. Move with purpose in reasonable time. Let your work be clean, your words be measured, your relationships be nurtured, and your life be deeply lived.

24 Because in the end, haste may make you fast—but it will also make waste.

Chapter 4

Nothing beats a failure but a try.

1 An extraordinary vocalist yearned to become a renown gospel recording artist. Though she happily performed at local churches and events, she greatly criticized her musical ability, spoke often of every risk of going further, and feared the unknown until the "what ifs" became tall walls of untouched potential, growing old under the safety of familiar dust. Her desire became a silent monument to a dream flattened, a certain failure born of not trying.

2 That's what happens with a lot of people. They don't lose because they tried and failed. They lose because they never try or they fail once and decide the story is over.

3 And I found that it's usually not the tried-and-failed stories that haunt people; it's what they never had the nerve to try that do.

4 Accomplishing things and achieving success take more than a longing. They take more than applause, talent, and good timing. They come from trying, layered with planning, practice, consistency, and perseverance.

5 Every builder knows the first crooked nail is not the end of the house. Every runner knows that stumbling out of the gate doesn't disqualify the finish.

6 The only true and certain failure is refusing to try.

7 The seed not planted can't yield a harvest, and the talent shut in cement can't bring increase.

8 My second son played Little League baseball. During one of his games, I watched a boy strike out in front of a packed crowd. His shoulders slumped as laughter rippled through the stands. The next inning, he walked back to the plate with the same bat, the same shaky knees, and a focused heart. This time, he connected. The ball didn't just clear the infield; it cleared the

fence. The crowd that had first laughed, stood up to cheer the loudest. What changed? Not the pitcher. Not the pressure. Just the courage to try and try again.

9 The hand that reaches forth, though it may tremble, pushes back the darkness of inaction.

10 The heart that decides to begin, though it may flinch, has already outdone the outcome of not having tried at all.

11 Trying is an act of quiet faith. It says, "This moment doesn't get the final word." It says, "This intent is worth my effort." It says, "I trust God to help me try."

12 Trying does not guarantee winning, but it always guarantees growth. You come back wiser. Stronger. More humble. More honest about where you shined and what you can improve on. Each attempt stretches your faith and straightens your spine.

13 And trust what I say, regret hits harder than failure because it has no proof, no data, no lesson—only a question mark that echoes in your heart for years.

14 So, don't fear a stumble or the possibility of falling short. Pick up your courage like a tool and take your best shot. In the very act of trying, you will defeat failure, past or future.

15 Why? Because nothing beats a failure but the stubborn decision to try or try again.

Chapter 5

Never be broke.

1 My dear mother taught me and my siblings to always keep a dollar. I learned the hard way what she meant.

2 I worked two jobs as a young husband and father to provide for my growing family. Full-time at the electrical plant making transformers and part-time at a grocery store. When the electrical plant had a lay off that included my job, I found work at the dog food plant until the layoff ended. I had no fears about working and working hard.

3 Even then, it was a mighty stretch to make what little pay I earned cover the basics—food on the table, gas in the car, shoes on growing feet—and still scrape

together enough for a small want now and then. Every dollar had an assignment before it ever reached my pocket.

4 Whenever my expenses ran faster in between paychecks than my dollars, it felt like life chose those moments to test every hinge and seam—the car's radiator, the washing machine, a child's wounded foot, the homeowners' insurance. All calling my name at once.

5 I would borrow from "Peter" to pay "Paul" which pushed me further into a red economic hole. (See Chapter 6 about avoiding this mistake.)

6 Whenever my money outlasted the month and I had a little something to set aside, nothing needed repair. Nothing was due.

7 That's when I learned why Mama would urge us to always keep a dollar. She was saying that having a dollar means you're still in the black; that you still have something in your hand to turn into something more; that you are not broke.

8 Being short on cash and being broke are not the same thing.

9 One is a circumstance of not having a lot of money which is a state of *what you're in*. It ebbs and flows and can change at any moment. The other is a condition

of your mind where you identify with poverty, meaning it is *what you are*.

10 Being broke almost guarantees you will stay short on money, because money is not drawn to a defeated mindset. Poverty first takes root in the mind before it shows up in the wallet. What you expect, you prepare for—and what you prepare for often becomes your reality.

11 Being broke is not just having an empty wallet. Being broke is having no cushion, no inventiveness, and no faith when life leans hard. And life will lean. It always does.

12 Yet a person who decides to never be broke invites money and wealth because that mindset guides what they keep, what they waste, and what they prepare for.

13 A "never be broke" mindset knows that there is dignity in restraint. It knows that there is power in margin. It knows that there is peace in preparation to be ready when the hard comes.

14 "Never be broke" means to not spend tomorrow's bread on today's appetite.

15 It is honoring what you have so you are not devastated by what you lack. It means learning to leave the store with something still in your pocket, even when the world says, "You deserve it." It means

understanding that every dollar is not just currency; it is a choice, a seed, a statement about what you believe about your future and what that future will require.

16 "Never be broke" means learning to live below your means even when your means begin to grow.

17 Too many people escape poverty only to be captured by lifestyle. The raise becomes a new car. The promotion becomes a larger house. The blessing becomes a burden. And suddenly, the income grew and the freedom disappeared.

18 "Never be broke" also means to not let yourself be empty—empty of vision, of courage, of aspiration.

19 This goes beyond money and the material. It's your awareness to build an inner abundance of resources, like ingenuity, generosity, resilience, and patience, with the power to change a short-on-cash situation into creativity, opportunity, and valuable skills. It ensures you are never depleted, always capable of innovating and rebuilding.

20 Rather than fear, "never be broke" is an attitude and a holy practice rooted in wisdom and godliness.

21 It is the quiet, defiant declaration of the poor, spoken again and again in faith: "I am rich." Not in what is seen, but in what is possible through discipline,

stewardship, trust in God, and the constant belief that lack will not have the final word.

Chapter 6

Don't borrow from "Peter" to pay "Paul".

1 Sometimes you may feel you have no choice but to borrow from "Peter" to pay "Paul" to get by.

2 I'm not talking about two men. I'm talking about a circular trap that looks like progress but keeps you standing in the same tired, penniless place. It is the illusion of movement without the dignity of advancement.

3 I know because I've been there and done that.

4 A credit card pays a utility bill. A loan covers the credit card. A second loan covers the first. The numbers move, but the stress stays and grows.

5 Because every dollar borrowed carries expectation. Every unpaid balance carries weight. And when you live from shift to shift, you squeeze your freedom to choose and breathe. You become reactive instead of intentional.

6 What begins as a solution becomes a cycle. And this cycle, if not broken, becomes a cage.

7 To borrow from one obligation to cover another is to shift pressure, not relieve it. The bill may be quiet for the moment, but the burden only changes shoulders. The anxiety simply moves from one room in the house to another. Today, it sits with Paul. Tomorrow, it lays with Peter. Either way, it still lives with you.

8 I learned from going through this that it's best to face what stands in front of you plainly, prayerfully, and steadily.

9 It is better to slow down than to stretch yourself thin, pretending you can outrun consequences.

10 Borrowing from Peter to pay Paul often grows out of embarrassment, impatience, or fear.

11 We don't want to be seen as struggling. We don't want to wait. We don't want to fall behind. But wisdom is not about appearance. Wisdom is about what you can bear.

12 Sometimes the bravest thing you can do is call a bill what it is and your bank account what it is, admitting that they disagree.

13 Then, turn your faith into a plan that brings the two into harmony. A smaller life for a season. A humbler choice. A disciplined pause. A debt rearrangement solution. A choice to not make tomorrow responsible for what today refuses to face, and to not stack pressure on pressure and call it progress.

14 Borrowing isn't always wrong. There are seasons when a wise loan can serve as a bridge, a tool, or a stepping-stone toward something better.

15 Yet borrowing without direction is dangerous. There is a world of difference between strategic support and survival swapping. One is guided by purpose and a plan. The other is driven by pressure and panic. One builds. The other barely balances.

16 Too many people live in a constant shuffle— moving money from *here* to cover *there*, shifting debt from one pocket to another, celebrating a temporary breath of relief while the deeper burden quietly grows.

17 Financial peace and freedom do not come from juggling debt with better hands. They come from breaking the pattern entirely. You cannot rearrange chains and call it liberty.

18 The first real break is always an honest look in the mirror.

19 It is the moment you stop blaming the economy, your upbringing, or bad luck, and begin to tell yourself the truth about your habits, your choices, and your patterns. After that comes the wise step of restraint—the courage to say "not this time," the humility to wait, the discipline to live within what you can truly carry.

20 Borrowing from Peter to pay Paul keeps you running in circles, feeling busy but going nowhere.

21 Wisdom calls you to stop running, stand still, and choose a different road—one marked by patience, planning, and faith that God's provision does not require you to stay trapped in the cycle of debt.

Chapter 7

Think twice, speak once.

1 One piece of advice I share often is to, "Think twice, speak once."

2 I like to think of it as a green light for the mind and a brake pedal for the mouth. And a piece of wisdom that many learn too late: words once released do not return politely to where they came from.

3 Thinking twice is both hesitation and honor. It is the discipline of letting a thought pass through discernment before it passes through the lips. It is the quiet humility of asking, *Is this true? Is this necessary? Is this kind? Is this the right moment?*

4 Because timing can turn medicine into poison just as easily as poison into medicine.

5 Speaking once means you recognize the finality of sound. Once spoken, words cannot be edited. They cannot be recalled. They land where they land and do what they do. You can apologize for a wound, but you cannot uncut the flesh.

6 Careless speech is like striking a match in a dry forest. You may not intend a fire, but fire is what you often get.

7 Sentences spoken too quickly can set homes ablaze. I've seen it happen.

8 Friendships can collapse under words that were meant as jokes. Careers often stall by a moment of quick honesty that forgot to be wise. And healing can begin with one thoughtful sentence spoken at exactly the right time. Same mouth. Same tongue. Different discipline.

9 Thinking twice is stewardship of thought. Your words are tools. In the right hands, they build, lift, repair, and guide. In the wrong moment they bruise, divide, destroy, and mislead. It's a difference of a pause rather than intention.

10 And contrary to what some folk think, silence is not weakness. Silence is strength under control. The

loudest person in the room is rarely the wisest, and the quickest answer is not always the truest or best one.

11 Wisdom walks slowly and speaks selectively.

12 As a pastor, there were times I could have corrected situations publicly but chose to wait and counsel privately. As a husband or parent, I could have reacted rashly but chose to respond after prayer. For me, it wasn't about being right or getting the long end of the stick. I valued peace and righteousness more important than proving any point.

13 Thinking twice is also an act of love.

14 Love cares how a word will land, not just how it feels to release it. Love understands that truth without timing can become cruelty. And kindness without truth can be fear. To think twice is to hold both in the same calm hand.

15 When you speak only after thinking twice, your words attract. People listen differently. They trust differently. They know that when you speak, something thoughtful is coming—not just something emotional. You begin to speak fewer words, but better ones. And better words shape better outcomes.

16 We live in a world that rewards instant reactions. Hot takes. Quick replies. Public opinions offered with

no private reflection. It makes some people feel smart and powerful.

17 But speed has never been the same as wisdom. Volume has never been the same as authority. And reaction has never been the same as response.

18 Thinking twice teaches patience with your own emotions. Speaking once teaches responsibility for your influence. Together they form a discipline that protects relationships, preserves dignity, and builds faith.

19 Think twice before you answer in anger. Think twice before you correct out loud. Think twice before you speak on matters you have not fully examined. Think twice before you let frustration choose your vocabulary.

20 Then, when you do speak—speak once. Speak clearly. Speak truthfully. Speak with intention. Speak to heal, not harm.

21 Because in the end, it's not how much you say that defines you. It's what survives after the echo fades.

22 Words fly fast and far, but only a few land with weight enough to leave a mark. Long after the conversation has ended and the room has grown quiet, what lingers is not the noise, but the truth.

23 People may forget the volume of your voice, but they will remember the spirit of your words.

24 I have found that the wisest words are the ones patient enough to be chosen.

25 They are not hurried out of impulse or emotion, but drawn up from reflection, prayer, and restraint. These words come seasoned, not raw. They comfort rather than inflame, clarify rather than confuse, and heal rather than wound. They do their work quietly, like seed planted deep in good soil.

26 Too many of us speak simply to be heard, to win, or to defend ourselves. But the person who thinks twice and speaks once speaks with intention.

27 So choose your words the way a craftsman chooses tools—carefully, purposefully, and with respect for the work ahead.

28 A few well-chosen words can build bridges, mend hearts, settle storms, and guide a life. Loud speech impresses for a moment. Wise speech—thought about twice and spoken once—shapes for a lifetime.

Chapter 8

You can do most anything for a short period of time.

1 There was a season when my finances were stretched thin as I supported my wife, our three young children, and a brand-new mortgage all at once.

2 I worked full-time, picked up a side job, and made the mistake of borrowing from "Peter" to pay "Paul." (I already talked about how that road ends in Chapter 6.) The pressure was heavy, and the climb felt steep.

3 To dig our way out, my wife, Zelda, and I made a clear agreement: a stop on unnecessary spending. No extras. No indulgences. Just discipline and determination.

4 I was blessed that Zelda and I saw eye-to-eye and walked together in harmony, especially on big things like finances. She put a halt to buying the fabric she loved to sew with and the jewelry she'd often pair with an older outfit. It wasn't easy, but it was necessary.

5 About three months into our spending fast, after paying our water bill one afternoon, she stepped into a department store "just to look around." Her eyes caught a pretty yellow hat. She tried it on. Took it off. Tried it on again. Then she put it back and walked out of the store without it. She honored our agreement even when nobody but God was watching.

6 That spending pause lasted about a year. And not long after, the brief, bitter trial gave way to the lasting reward of financial peace and freedom. That yellow hat was forgotten. And though the top shelf of her closet became full of hats, Zelda never again desired or owned a yellow one.

7 That season taught us something permanent: the ability to take on temporary discomfort is a foundation for achieving any noble aspiration. Whether it is a long night to master a skill, discipline to save for a dream, or laser focus to complete a life-changing work—what makes the load bearable is knowing it is not forever.

8 This mindset turns overwhelming challenges into manageable sprints. The difficulty is not denied, but its duration is contained. Its purpose is magnified by the

vision of what waits on the other side. That's the holy trade that turns short-term sacrifice into long-term victory.

9 So bow your neck for a season. Tighten your belt for a while. Say "no" now so you can say "yes" later. Put your head down, square your shoulders, and get to work.

10 If truth be told—and I'm about to tell it—you really can do most anything for a short period of time.

Chapter 9

Be careful who you hang around. In just a little while, you will become like them and do what they do.

1 Choose your circle with fierce intention because their echoes will soon become your own voice.

2 In a little while with them, you will start to sound like them, think like them, and eventually do what they do. That is not a threat; it's simply how influence works.

3 The company you keep is not just companionship; it's quiet assimilation. Little by little, without any announcement, your habits begin to shift. Your

language changes. Your standards bend. Your dreams either sharpen or shrink.

4 Why? Because habits, mindsets, and ambitions are contagious.

5 Just as laughter spreads in a room, so do bitterness, laziness, courage, discipline, faith, and vision.

6 Proximity is powerful.

7 Whatever spirit you sit beside long enough will eventually introduce itself in your own behavior. Whether the traits around you are lifting and life-giving or heavy and limiting, they will seep into your subconscious and shape the way you move through the world. Before long, you will find yourself mirroring attitudes you once only observed.

8 Your future self is being sculpted by the hands you hold today. Every lunch table, every phone call, every late-night conversation is quietly voting on who you are becoming.

9 So look for people who stretch you toward your higher self. Walk with those who pray when life gets hard, who work when things get slow, who tell the truth when it would be easier to flatter. Connect with those who live the values you aspire to carry.

9 Because this much is certain: You don't just keep company. In time, you become it.

Chapter 10

Stand for the truth, even if you must stand alone.

1 Truth is not simply a fact to be proven or an opinion to be defended.

2 Truth is the very essence and self-expression of Creator God.

3 Truth is what *is*—steady, unflinching, and unchanged by popular vote. Facts can shift with new information, but truth stands even when the lights go out and the crowd goes home.

4 To stand for what you know to be true, especially when the path feels lonely, is an act of enduring integrity and profound self-respect.

5 It's also a form of holy courage. Anyone can stand when surrounded by applause. It takes a rooted soul to stand when the room grows quiet and the support slips away.

6 Standing for truth will not always make you popular. The crowd may sway. Voices may cry for compromise. The warmth of agreement may tempt you to soften your stance just enough to fit in. But fitting in has never been the same as standing tall. And being liked has never been the same as being right.

7 When you choose truth, you honor not only God, but your own conscience. And though it may feel at times like you are standing by yourself, your obedience becomes a quiet beacon for others who are watching from a distance, trying to find their own courage.

8 You may never know who gathers strength simply because you refused to bend to popular lies.

9 Fear not the silence that sometimes accompanies standing alone. Fear instead the hollowness that settles into a life that has learned to betray itself for comfort or approval.

10 There is no possession more costly than a surrendered conviction.

11 Support the truth when it whispers. Stand for the truth when it is shouted down. And when the hour of decision arrives—and it surely will—choose truth over ease, truth over applause, truth over safety.

12 Because every generation is tested not by how loudly it speaks, but by what it refuses to deny.

13 And every life is finally measured not by how often it agreed, but by what it would not let go.

14 Stand for the truth, even if you must stand alone.

Chapter 11

The truth crushed to the ground will rise again.

1 Truth has a bruising history.

2 It has been ignored, denied, buried, shouted down, and pressed flat beneath the weight of convenience and power.

3 Still, it rises. Always. You can push it into the dirt, but you cannot keep it there. Truth has resurrection in its bones.

4 There are seasons when lies wear fine suits and walk confidently through the world, while truth limps

behind, wounded and mocked. In those moments, it looks as if injustice has won, as if deception has the final word. But history and life teach otherwise.

5 The lie always runs fast at first. The truth moves slower, but it never stops.

6 I have seen truth mistreated in families, buried under pride and silence. I have seen it mishandled in churches, pushed aside for comfort and order. I have seen it denied in business, in courts, in friendships, and in hearts too afraid to face what honesty would demand. For a while, the lie stands tall. For a while. But only for a while.

7 Truth is like a seed.

8 You can stomp on the ground where it lies, sure you have crushed it for good. But underground, where no applause follows, that seed is breaking open. Pressure does not destroy it; it prepares it. Time does not silence it; it strengthens it.

9 And when truth rises, it does not ask permission.

10 In the fullness of time, the day comes when what was hidden demands air. What was denied insists on being named. What was twisted straightens itself. And in that moment, people often say, "I always knew." The truth had been speaking the whole time. It was only waiting for a hearing.

11 This is why I say in Chapter 10 that standing with truth matters, even when it falls and bleeds in your hands. Even when it costs you friends, position, or comfort. Even when the crowd swears that truth is outdated, too sharp, too inconvenient.

12 The ground has never been a grave for truth—only a womb.

13 Some of the hardest moments in life come when the truth rises and exposes what we hoped would stay buried. But exposure is an invitation to heal. To repent. To rebuild on something solid at last.

14 Truth may be crushed by rumor. It may be pushed down by power. It may be covered by fear.

15 But truth carries the breath of God in it. And whatever carries God's breath cannot stay underground forever.

16 Do not be discouraged when truth seems defeated. Do not mistake its silence for surrender. Do not confuse delay with death.

17 Truth is patient. Truth is stubborn. Truth knows the way back to the light.

18 Align your life with it. Speak it when it's costly. Live it when it's lonely. Trust it when it looks like it has lost.

19 Why? Because in the end, after the dust settles and the noise fades, one thing remains certain: the truth—no matter how badly it is crushed—will rise again.

Chapter 12

What you can't do, the Most High God can.

1 The year was 1972. I had not yet been a full year at the helm of Shiloh Baptist Church—the church I would pastor for nearly fifty years—when the deacons responded to my vision for a new church with their doubts about our ability to build a much-needed new home.

2 The old, wood-framed building had stood for some fifty years before I ever arrived. Time had softened it to a weary, silvery gray beneath layers of peeling white paint. Cracks in the side boards welcomed warm summer breezes and cold winter winds alike. The

foundation—an uneven stacking of fieldstones that shifted with the earth—held up the vestibule, sanctuary, pulpit, choir stand with its upright piano, and a few small rooms tucked behind.

3 Outdoor plumbing tested both patience and courage. More than once, a visitor was greeted by a critter that challenged one's resolve to really "go." And baptisms? Those only happened in warm weather when the outdoor pool was fit for holy use.

4 One day the older men said to me, "We've been here all these years and haven't been able to build. What makes you think you can build a new church with these poor folks and this little money?"

5 "I can't," I replied in my simple truth. "But the God I serve can."

6 Three years later, by faith in that Most High power—and by our aligning our actions with what we believed—I led the congregation into a new, brick, two-story building with indoor plumbing, modern amenities, and space to grow.

7 What stood before us had once seemed impossible. But God had already made room for it.

8 Similarly, my oldest grandson came to me one day with what he described as a seemingly impossible task: finding his soulmate, a fitting young lady to walk

with him in life. He had looked and waited, dated and been disappointed, and grown weary. Like so many before him, he had reached the end of what he could control. I listened carefully, then smiled, knowing that his faith was about to be tested.

9 "You can't make that happen," I started, "But God can."

10 I reminded him that a good marriage is not hunted down like prey but prepared for like a harvest.

11 We spoke of him going into sincere prayer to ask God to point him in the right direction. We talked about him being the kind of man worthy of the woman he was praying for—strong in character, faithful in spirit, disciplined in purpose. Then we prayed together, not for speed, but for alignment.

12 In about five weeks, quietly and without fanfare, God did what God does best. Through an ordinary introduction by a friend and an unremarkable moment, a remarkable connection was made. Today, that once "impossible" request is now a living testimony seated at family tables and walking through life at my grandson's side—married and blessed parents to my three great-grandchildren.

13 Once again, I saw it clearly: when human effort reaches its limit, Heaven steps in.

14 Dream big, but dream in harmony with God. Ask the Lord to direct your steps toward the vision. Write it down. Speak it plainly to yourself and to a few faithful people who will pray with you and labor beside you. Then do all that your hands can do.

15 And when you reach the edge of what your strength can manage, stop worrying about what you cannot do.

16 Because what you cannot do, the Most High God can. And often does—right on time. You only believe.

Chapter 13

Can't nobody tell you anything, but just wait awhile and you'll soon see [that what I'm telling you is true].

1 When we are in our teens and twenties, we often believe we know enough to run the world.

2 Strength is new. Confidence is loud. Experience feels overrated. Advice sounds like interference. And so, with full hearts and short sight, we press forward certain that our way is the best way.

3 Rather than heed the counsel of those who have already traveled the road we're eager to speed down, pride persuades us to dismiss their wisdom.

4 Knowledge offered is mistaken for control. Correction feels like criticism. And what might have saved us time and trouble is brushed aside as outdated.

5 So, we remain ignorant. Not because wisdom was unavailable, but because we refused to receive it.

6 Then life steps in as teacher.

7 Only later, when the contests of life rise up and test our resolve—when partnerships strain, money tightens, health falters, or plans fall apart—does the one who "knew everything" begin to hear differently.

8 In the stillness of consequence, we remember the quiet words spoken by an elder long ago. And with humbled eyes we finally see that the tried-and-tested wisdom we once ignored was steady, sound, and true.

9 Time has a way of tutoring what pride refuses to learn.

10 The lesson is simple yet demanding: stay open. Stay pliable. Let yourself be taught. Especially by those who have already borne the weight you are just beginning to lift.

11 Position yourself near people who have scars and not just opinions, stories and not just theories, endurance and not just energy.

12 Be slow to dismiss wisdom that is unfamiliar to you.

13 What you don't yet understand may be the very thing that saves you years of heartache, wasted effort, and costly detours. There is always more to know than what you currently know. And God often hides that knowledge in the lived experience of others.

14 You don't have to learn everything the hard way. Some lessons can be borrowed.

15 But if you won't listen now, just wait awhile—life will repeat the truth in a louder voice.

Chapter 14

Ease your hand out of the lion's mouth.

1 There will come a day when you find yourself in a risky situation. It may look good on the outside and feel dangerous on the inside.

2 It might be a high-paying, important job that is quietly ruining your mental and physical health. A draining friendship filled with unending fuss and little true support. A failing business venture you keep propping up with borrowed hope. Or some other tight place that has closed its teeth around you.

3 It will feel as though your hand is stuck in a lion's mouth.

4 What you must not do is panic and try to snatch your hand back with all your might.

5 Panic makes people storm into offices and quit in anger. Panic turns hard conversations into explosions. Panic makes desperate gamblers out of thoughtful builders. Sudden movements invite sudden damage.

6 That kind of yank can cost you your livelihood, your reputation, your peace, and sometimes relationships that might have ended more gently. A sudden pull invites a hard bite.

7 No—be wise and stay calm. Humble yourself. Pray. Breathe. Think.

8 Then, little by little, begin to ease your hand out so lightly the lion barely notices.

9 If it's a job, make a quiet plan. Begin networking over coffee. Take informational interviews during lunch breaks. Prepare a soft landing before you leave hard ground.

10 If it's a friendship, create loving boundaries that restore balance instead of igniting war.

11 If it's a business, stop throwing good money after bad. Scale down. Pivot if possible. Or prepare for an orderly ending.

12 The goal is not to tame the lion or prove your bravery. The goal is to walk away with your whole life intact—your peace, your integrity, your future, and your relationships.

13 Some escapes require shouting. But most deliverance comes quietly.

14 Ease your hand out of the lion's mouth with wisdom, patience, and grace.

Chapter 15

Strike while the iron is hot.

1 When I was a young man working down at the Puritan Cordage Mill, some of the old Black men would often swap stories about the remarkable skill of blacksmiths—some enslaved, some newly freed— whose talent they had witnessed or heard passed down through family and time.

2 "Bennie down dere off Reese Street knew how to hit dat metal wit dat hamma at jus da right time, when dat iron was red like fire," one would say. "He'd ben dat iron into somethin' you could use. Ah farm tool or a nice rail. And when dat heat got cool, it got hard and strong." They would laugh, slap their knees, and nod

their heads with pride, as if they could still hear the ring of hammer on metal.

3 Their joy in that fine craft stayed with me. And over time, it shaped how I came to understand life.

4 A blacksmith must know when to strike. Too soon, and the work is wasted. Too late, and the iron has hardened beyond shaping. The power is not just in the strength of the blow; it is in the timing.

5 So it is with opportunity.

6 Opportunities, like heated iron, do not remain hot and bendy forever. They pass or they harden. A door opens, a window lifts, a moment presents itself.

7 If you recognize it and move with courage and wisdom, something useful and lasting can be forged. If you hesitate too long, that same moment may cool and close.

8 A job opening. A new relationship. A call to step into leadership. An idea worth pursuing. Each has its season of readiness. Success often depends less on raw talent and more on whether you can discern when the iron is truly hot.

9 Too often, hesitation born of fear, doubt, or the comfort of routine allows the chance to slip away. We tell ourselves we'll act later—when we feel safer, when

we feel more ready, when life feels less demanding. But later is not always promised.

10 Still, striking does not mean rushing. The blacksmith does not swing wildly. The work calls for wisdom as much as boldness, preparation, discipline, patience, and attentiveness. You must tend the fire long before the iron glows. You must be ready before the moment arrives.

11 The lesson is this: stay prepared, so when God heats the iron of opportunity in your life, you are not scrambling for the hammer.

12 Then, strike with faith. Strike with wisdom. Strike while the iron is hot.

Chapter 16

Things don't just happen; they're made to happen.

1 Nothing we see in this world appears by accident.

2 There's no such thing as luck—good or bad—and no such thing as coincidence. What we often call chance is usually the hidden meeting place of purpose and preparation.

3 Everything—from inventions and breakthroughs to hellos and goodbyes—is made to happen through thought. An ask or a desire expressed as prayer, imagination tempered by discipline, effort guided by faith, patience strengthened by persistence.

4 It is like the farmer who plants a seed hoping for a harvest. Hopeful thought compels action. He tills the soil. He waters the seed and pulls weeds. And then, after all the human work is done, the farmer still trusts the workings of God for the increase. The harvest is not an accident. It is the fruit of partnership.

5 Each of us, whether we realize it or not, is a participant in a holy collaboration with God in what unfolds in our lives. Good or not so good. Heaven supplies the power of the *how*. You supply the spark of the *what*.

6 My children once rode the bus to their integrated elementary school. The bus patrol made the Black children sit in the back. When my wife and I learned what was happening, I gathered a group of parents and we went before the Board of Education to lodge a formal complaint. The very next day, our children were allowed to sit anywhere they chose. That change did not happen by accident. It was made to happen—by awareness, courage, action, and faith.

7 My two youngest children are eighteen months apart in age. Later in life, the season came when I was responsible for paying college tuition for both of them at the same time. My wife and I carried that load with joy, but also with genuine prayer, asking God to help us meet the need. One week after my daughter began her freshman year, she received a letter congratulating her on being awarded the Harry Loef Scholarship,

covering all four years of her undergraduate education. She had not applied. Her mother and I had not applied. Someone whose name we never learned had nominated her. That blessing had hands behind it and prayer beneath it.

8 Every summer for some fifteen years, my wife, our three children, and their families vacationed together for about a week. Yes, everyone had tight schedules. Jobs made demands. School calendars had their say. Babies were coming, bills were due, and life was busy in all the ways life is always busy. Still, we chose one week and *made it happen*. Those weeks did not just fall out of the sky. They were built with intention, protected with commitment, and sustained by shared priority. And now, years later, they live on as some of our family's most treasured memories. Time together did not *happen* to us—we *made it happen*. And in making it, we made something lasting.

9 These are only three of the many times I witnessed this truth firsthand—that outcomes, that what we experience don't just happen; they are made to happen by our holy collaboration.

10 Every act—active or passive, conscious or unconscious—produces after its kind, like a seed. Not by force, but in harmony with God's unshakable laws.

11 So the call is clear: be an intentional maker. Shape your days with purpose. Pray over what you pursue.

Act on what you believe. Conduct yourself as a participant in the workings of Heaven, instead of a spectator waiting for whatever comes.

12 Because things don't just happen; they are made to happen.

Chapter 17

Prepare for war in time of peace.

1 Scripture and history both teach us that life moves in seasons.

2 "There is a time of war and a time of peace," Ecclesiastes tells us. Which means peace, as precious as it is, is not meant to be mistaken for permanence.

3 In every life, "war" seasons will come—sickness, grief, financial hardship, betrayal, loss, injustice— often without warning and rarely by appointment.

4 The only real question is not *if* they will come, but how prepared you will be when they do.

5 To prepare for war in a time of peace is a call to holy readiness while the waters are still calm. This is the season to strengthen the boat—not when the storm clouds are already rolling in. This is the hour for quiet, intentional work that no one applauds but everyone benefits from later.

6 Peace is the time to fortify your spirit with prayer and understanding. It is the time to shape your character *before* it is tested.

7 Peace is the season to tend your relationships while love flows easily, to order your finances while the bills are manageable, to discipline your mind and body while strength still feels natural.

8 What you build in peace is what will hold you in war—when sickness comes unannounced, when grief knocks the wind out of you, when a job is lost, when relationships rupture, when the ground shifts beneath plans you thought were solid.

9 The prayers you whispered in calm seasons will speak for you when your own words fail. The savings you stacked quietly will steady you when income stops. The friendships you nurtured in joy will carry you through sorrow. The discipline you practiced in daylight will guide you through the darkest nights.

10 Peace-time choices become war-time shelter.

11 Do not squander peacetime on carelessness or complacency. Honor it. Treasure it. Invest it. Because when the battle comes, it will not ask whether you are ready. It will simply reveal whether you are.

12 When you use peace wisely, you meet wartime with clarity instead of panic, with courage instead of despair, with strength instead of weakness.

13 Peace, then, is not merely a pause between troubles. Peace is sacred preparation. Use it well.

Chapter 18

It takes two fools to fight.

1 A fight is like two drunks arguing over the last drop—messy, loud, and nobody really wins.

2 It's like two blind men swinging at each other in the street—everybody watching sees the comedy, but nobody sees the sense.

3 If the truth were told—and I'm about to tell it—a fight never happens with just one person. It takes two fearful minds, two hot tempers, and two hearts unwilling to listen and too quick to strike.

4 It takes two fools to fight.

5 Foolish conflict is less about truth and more about pride. It is the fragile ego, not faithful conviction, looking for a stage.

6 Pride wants to be right, to win the moment.

7 Yet, the wise one knows better.

8 The wise one—seeking to save the relationship, the reputation, and the soul—knows when to walk away because every battle is not worth the bruises it leaves behind.

9 Wisdom, wanting to be whole, knows that refusing to engage doesn't make you weak; it makes you free.

10 Wisdom knows that one voice shouting into silence eventually runs out of power.

11 Wisdom knows that real strength is restraint, and real victory is peace. Because peace does not need proof, but pride always does.

12 Wisdom also knows that anger is expensive. It charges you your joy, your clarity, your health, and sometimes your future.

13 Many have lost more by winning an argument than they ever would have lost by letting one go.

14 To disengage from foolish conflict is not cowardice; it is consecration. It is choosing composure over chaos, purpose over performance.

15 You don't wrestle with pigs unless you want to get muddy, and you don't argue with fools unless you want to look like one. You would do best to preserve your energy for building, not breaking.

16 It takes two fools to fight, but it takes only one wise soul to end it.

Chapter 19

A scared man can't win.

1 A tall, broad-shouldered man from our Baptist association reluctantly agreed to present our small group's recommendation before the full body—about four hundred watchful faces.

2 When the time came, the weight of the task dragged along as he made a slow walk to the stage. The paper in his hand trembled like a leaf in a quiet storm. He gripped it tighter, cleared his throat, and opened his mouth to speak. But all that came out was, "Ah… ah… ah."

3 The silence that followed was thick enough to cut with a knife until a wave of "go 'heads" and

"amens"—part sympathy, part suspense—tried to will his courage to return.

4 Fear will make a grown man forget his name and how to read. I saw it happen many times.

5 Fear will cause the noblest of people to shrink their vision, hide their gifts, or run from blessings they prayed mightily for like a wild rabbit fleeing a hungry fox.

6 When fear takes over, clear thinking flies out the window.

7 That's why the old folks said, "A scared man can't win."

8 You can't conquer what you're too afraid to see and face.

9 You can't receive what you're too nervous to reach for, to hold to.

10 The scared person, busy imagining defeat, studies the mountain while the fearless one starts climbing, too focused on destiny to back down without taking a chance.

11 If you're like me, you might have your own story about that truth.

12 I was actively involved in the nearby church of my youth and young manhood, always willing to serve wherever a hand was needed. The congregants began to notice that whenever a problem arose, "'Ol Burn"— what they called me—was diligent not only to name it but to offer a solution.

13 In time, when the position of Chairman of the Deacon's Board became vacant, they voted me into the role. It was no small thing. Seniority traditionally carried great weight in such decisions, and several deacons were older and had served far longer than I. Some were angry at the outcome. Still, I accepted the responsibility without fear, doing what I had already been doing—serving my community with faith, integrity, and a continuing commitment to move forward the work of God.

14 That's how I know that winning begins in your mind, long before any battle or challenge or task ever knocks on your door.

15 You decide ahead of time: flee like the rabbit or be courageous enough to move forward anyway, trusting that alignment with God is greater than your shaking knees.

16 If truth be told—and I'm about to tell it—fear and faith cannot take up the same space. The one you choose will rise, and the other will disappear.

17 When what you are doing is in sync with God, then there is no need to fear.

18 Why? Because the Spirit of God in you does not tremble; it conquers.

19 A scared man can't win, but a Spirit-led one can't lose.

Chapter 20

If a man is not careful, he will destroy himself.

1 It's rare that you find someone who wants to destroy himself or herself.

2 Most of us want to enjoy prosperity of good living with health, family, community, long life, and money.

3 Yet and still, not everyone is willing to match their words and deeds to that ideal and not every downfall is from the devil.

4 If you're not watchful of your thoughts and habits, you will destroy yourself—slowly, silently, smiling all the while.

5 It is usually not all at once in one big mistake, but little by little through a thousand small ones. Through the lie he tells himself in secret. Through the ask she's too proud to pray for. Through the wisdom he's too stubborn to hear. Through her every compromise of character.

6 It happens through calling fear "wisdom" and pride "strength." Through shortcuts taken and grudges nursed. Through a solo journey that leaves God on the sidelines.

7 But hear me—carefulness is spiritual alertness. It is staying awake to the choices that shape your soul.

8 It is knowing that the same fire that warms you can also burn you if you stop paying attention.

9 The same water that keeps you alive can also drown you if you fail to see what is happening.

10 Your foes don't need to wear you down if you do it to yourself.

11 So, check that you are building yourself up. Guard your mind and motives. Watch your steps. Stay humble enough to be corrected.

The Book of BURNETT

Chapter 21

Don't take no wooden nickels.

1 When I was young and heading out of the house, my father would often call after me with a grin and a knowing shake of his head, "Boy, don't take no wooden nickels." He wasn't merely talking about phony money.

2 He was teaching me how to move through the world with discernment. What he meant was simple and sacred: don't let nobody play you.

3 Life is full of counterfeits. You will meet fake friends with genuine smiles, false promises wrapped in fine words, and glitter that is not gold. You will encounter deals that look too good to be true because they are, and people who offer quick gain at the slow cost of your character.

4 There is a kind of pretense that flatters loudly but bonds shallow. It promises big and delivers small. It arrives dressed like a blessing but leaves like a burden. It shows up free, but without favor.

5 A wooden nickel looks real at first glance. It has shape, weight, and markings. But when put to use, it fails every test that matters.

6 So it is with shallow opportunity, dishonest relationships, and shortcuts that ask you to abandon your values. They may feel good in your hand for a moment, but they will not spend when life comes to collect.

7 Wisdom is knowing the difference between what shines and what is solid. It is learning to pause before you accept what is offered, to listen deeper than the sales pitch, and to weigh not only what you gain but what you might lose.

8 What I learned is never to trade my peace for approval, my truth for applause, or my integrity for

attention. Some things cost too much even when the price looks small.

9 Keep your eyes open and your spirit sharp. Not everything that comes smiling is sent to serve you. And yes, not everything that glitters is gold. Some things come to test your judgment, your patience, and your self-worth.

10 The world will hand you many wooden nickels. Take none of them. Carry only what is real, weighty, and true—for those are the riches that never fail you.

Chapter 22

What's worse than a young fool is an old fool.

1 Deacon John swore up and down that he still "had it." Eighty-seven years old, knees clicking like crickets, but he insisted that he could still outrun any man on the block. One day at the church picnic, he got to boasting, talking slick, and puffing his chest, saying, "Don't let the gray fool you, son. I still got wheels."

2 Brother Curtis, half John's age and twice his sense, chuckled and said, "Alright then, Deek. Let's see what cha got."

3 Before anyone could protest, John took off running across the lawn, t-shirt flapping like a flag of courage.

4 He made it about three car lengths before gravity and arthritis teamed up. Down he went. The saints ran over, helping him up, fanning him and praying, while he groaned, "I *told* y'all I still had it. I just didn't know where I put it."

5 We laughed and thanked God that he was okay. But the lesson was clear. Age doesn't guarantee wisdom any more than height guarantees maturity.

6 Some lessons can sit on a man's doorstep for decades and he still won't open the door. Some folks, a long time out of college, still act like freshmen chasing the next party. Some people outgrow foolishness; others just get older doing the same thing.

7 A young fool, we expect. Youth stumbles. Youth tries too hard or not at all. Youth believes it's invisible, invincible, and unbreakable.

8 A young fool spends money fast and speaks even faster, and only realizes the consequences of both once they've caught up with him. We shake our heads, offer a warning, maybe even a little grace, because youth is the classroom where you're *supposed* to learn.

9 But an old fool is a different kind of sorrow because nothing looks sadder than a grown person still tripping over lessons they were meant to learn years ago.

10 An old fool has had chances, usually many, to grow up and grow wise. He's lived through storms, heartbreaks, layoffs, betrayals, and blessings. He's heard no's that made him sit down and yes's that made him stand tall. Life has whispered in his ear, shouted from rooftops, and sometimes screamed in the night.

11 In fact, I've given wisdom to people who preferred their foolishness.

12 The barrier to wisdom and maturity is not a lack of experience. It's a lack of understanding.

13 A young fool wastes time by accident. An old fool wastes time on purpose.

14 A young fool mistakes noise for power. An old fool should know that quiet is where real strength lives.

15 A young fool doesn't yet understand who he is. An old fool refuses to do so.

16 Age should bring perspective, like stepping back from a newly painted room and finally seeing how the whole house holds together. You start noticing where you rushed a repair, where you steadied the front porch just right, where a wall color needed more courage, or

where the curtains kissed the floor at just the right length. Wisdom isn't measured by how many years you've lived or how many rooms you've built, but by how deeply you've paid attention along the way.

17 What makes an old fool worse is that his foolishness ripples.

18 A young fool mainly threatens his own future. An old fool is a danger to the futures of everyone who trusts him: his spouse, children, business partners, members of the community.

19 A young fool can say, "I didn't know." An old fool is left with saying, "I knew, but I didn't change."

20 The good news is that foolishness is not a life sentence.

21 Age may be stubborn, but change is available to anyone brave enough to face himself in the mirror— the one that reflects your patterns, decisions, habits, excuses, consistency, or lack thereof. That mirror doesn't lie, and it doesn't try to make you feel good. But it will improve the course of your life if you want it. If you let it.

22 What's worse than a young fool is an old fool. And what's better than either is the person—young or old— who finally decides to grow up.

23 So don't just count your years. *Weigh* them. Let every season teach you something so that you become wiser.

Chapter 23

You can't beat them at their own game.

1 I liked to go to the neighborhood fair when I was young to watch people play the shell game. The gamer used three walnut shells to hide a pea and after moving the shells around, the player had to guess which shell the pea was under. It was fun to see the good guesses by player after player fall flat, knowing that would never be me because I refused to play such a rigged game. A clever hand by the operator made it almost impossible to find the "missing pea".

2 It taught me that you can't beat anybody at their own game of deception, manipulation, domination, smooth

talking, or shaky moral shifting built and run with one winner in mind, and it isn't you.

3 Such people rewrite the rules mid-play to keep themselves on top.

4 The person who lives cunningly practices their moves for a long time. In their own game—whether its gambling, corrupt politics, or any other mischief—they are way ahead of any victim, intended or not.

5 They can lie faster than you can blink, twist the truth before you catch your breath, and walk away clean while you're scratching your head trying to figure out what happened.

6 If you try to beat them at that, you only dirty your own hands. And what good is victory if you must lose yourself to get it?

7 A man's strength is in how deeply he stands in the truth of who he is, rather than stooping to match the madness of a con man.

8 The moment you abandon your values to win, you've already been defeated by the trickster you were hoping to outthink. You've hopped into a ring where the cost of admission is your own character.

9 Trying to beat someone at their own game is like stepping into quicksand thinking you'll outrun it. The more you fight on their terms, the faster you sink.

10 So, what do you do when you encounter those folks—the ones who bend every rule but their own, who talk out of both sides of their mouth, who see people not as souls but as stones to step on? You don't try to beat them. You rise above them.

11 You walk in a higher wisdom, a quieter confidence, a slower, deeper breath. You let your integrity—not cheap gaming—do the talking.

12 You win the victory by refusing to lower your energy, rather than matching theirs. And stand tall.

13 Choose the path where your sleep is peaceful, your conscience is clear, and your name stays clean. Let those who live by schemes stay trapped in their own maze. You? Walk free.

Chapter 24

Like a Boy Scout, be ready at all times.

1 There's an old motto the Boy Scouts used to say with their chests lifted high: "Be prepared." Simple words, but a whole sermon lives inside them.

2 The tests of life knock on your door unannounced. Trouble comes without a summons. Opportunity pops up whether your shirt is ironed, shoes are shined, or your resume is current. And God may drop an assignment on you that's void of clear instructions.

3 The question then becomes, *Are you ready?*

4 Not ready in the sense of having every answer, but ready in the sense of being awake, alert, and anchored. Ready in your soul, your mind, and your character. Ready for what life might ask of you today, instead of someday.

5 When I think of readiness, I don't picture a soldier in full armor or a businessperson with a leather briefcase.

6 I picture a young Scout with a pocketknife his daddy gave him, a canteen on his hip, and a budding confidence in his step. He doesn't know what the trail will hold, but he knows what he carries. He knows what he's practiced. He knows what he's trained for. He knows who he is.

7 That's what readiness is: a trained spirit, not a perfect plan.

8 Readiness is built long before the moment you need it.

9 You store it every time you show up when you're tired, listen when your ego wants to talk, apologize when you'd rather defend yourself, save when you'd rather spend, walk away from foolishness when your pride wants to stay. Each such choice becomes a tool in your backpack.

10 And one day, you'll reach for exactly what you need, and you'll have it.

11 Or as my brother in the funeral business always said, "It's better to have and not need than to need and not have." That's readiness.

12 But if you live carelessly, reacting instead of preparing, drifting instead of learning, procrastinating instead of practicing, then you'll reach into that same backpack and find it empty.

13 Life has a way of revealing your preparation, your character, your decision making, your self-respect at the worst possible moment.

14 The unprepared person always looks surprised. The prepared person always looks steady.

15 Whatever you're praying for, prepare to rise to its level of habits, discipline, maturity, and accountability *before* it shows up.

16 Why? Because God does not give new keys to someone who's still losing the old ones. Preparation is how you tell Heaven, "I'm ready for more."

17 The same applies to your spiritual side. You can't walk through this world without facing seasons that shake you through events like sickness, betrayal, financial drought, and unexpected loss. Those moments don't suddenly create faith; they reveal the faith you've been either cultivating or neglecting all along. In spending time with God in the quiet hours to

be ready when things are loud and stormy. In learning to trust God in the small things to not fall apart in the big ones.

18 To be ready at all times means you have made quiet, faithful daily deposits in the bank of your soul—through prayer, discipline, learning, integrity, and spiritual alignment—so that when the moment comes, you are not scrambling for strength you should have already stored.

19 Being ready at all times also means practicing responsibility.

20 It's vital preparation that honors your commitments before they demand your attention.

21 If you know a bill is coming, don't scramble at the last minute—plan, save, and position yourself so you can meet your obligations without stress or compromise.

22 If you promised someone your time, arrive ready to give it fully, without distraction or complaint, respecting the value of both your word and theirs.

23 When raising children, readiness means shaping their hearts, minds, and character now, providing guidance, discipline, and example, so the world doesn't have to correct what you neglected.

24 Readiness is not passive. It is active, intentional, and daily. It's about showing up consistently, preparing quietly, and doing the work that ensures when opportunity, challenge, or responsibility appears, you are equipped, capable, and steadfast.

25 Basically, readiness is good stewardship for life as it comes.

26 So, like a Boy Scout, be ready at all times—not because fear drives you, but because wisdom guides you.

Chapter 25

There is plenty of room at the top.

1 Some people choke their own dreams because they believe the lie that success is scarce.

2 They act like the top is a crowded attic with one dusty chair and a single bare light bulb swinging in the dark. They think if someone else gets ahead, their own chances shrink.

3 If the truth were told—and I'm about to tell it—the top is not crowded. The top is wide open. And there is more than enough room for you.

4 I know that God doesn't do scarcity.

5 Most people don't believe that truth because they never climb high enough to see it.

6 The crowd is at the bottom where everyone is pushing and shoving for attention, complaining about what they can't have, or waiting for someone else to make a way for them.

7 Down there, envy grows like weeds, and comparison nips at your heels.

8 Down there, fear tells you to stay where it's familiar, even if familiar is suffocating.

9 Down there, to win means somebody else must lose so competition is cutthroat and keeps folks crawling in circles instead of climbing higher.

10 But the higher you do go—through vision, strategy, discipline, courage, adaption, faith, steadiness, and similar traits—the more space you find. The air thins out not because the world is short on greatness but because so few people choose the climb. Because too many people are still waiting for permission to rise.

11 Not everyone is willing to humble themselves and trade ego for growth. Not everyone is willing to forgo comfort for calling. Not everyone is willing to obey God's nudge when it leads beyond their excuses. Not everyone is willing to do what's required to climb.

12 When I say there is plenty of room at the top, I'm talking about two vital aspects of your life.

13 I'm talking about the top of your career, whatever that is—preacher, janitor, teacher, lawyer, painter, doctor, musician, or what have you. It's about excelling in your skill and knowledge in ways that advance you, provide for you, and fulfill you.

14 *And* I'm talking about the top of your spiritual being. This is about living fully, operating faithfully, and standing firmly in the purpose or place or desire God carved into your bones.

15 At this peak, titles don't matter. Getting here is measured solely by the fruit of your life, like peace, joy, integrity, self-love, freedom, and service to others.

16 God didn't make your light to dim mine, or mine to overshadow yours.

17 When you walk in your lane, on your mission, in your truth, you will find that no one else was built to stand exactly where you're standing.

18 The top becomes crowded only when you try to live someone else's life.

19 There are no lack of ideas, opportunities, resources, or ways to rise in being who you are. You'll find doors

opening you didn't even know existed all because you live the truth of you.

20 Also know that people who reach the top never try to push others down. That kind of insecurity lives only halfway up the mountain where you're still performing, still comparing, still proving something to somebody who doesn't matter.

21 The ones standing fully in who they are, are too busy elevating others to be threatened by them. They know what it cost to get there, and they know the world is better when more people rise.

22 But here's an important point: the climb is optional.

23 Nobody carries you. Nobody drags you. Nobody pushes you past your own willingness.

24 You lace up your own shoes, pack your character, prepare your mind, and step upward even when the trail feels steep.

25 Every step you take over every temptation resisted, on every lesson learned, by every discipline chosen creates more space around you. It lifts you above pettiness, mediocrity, and noise.

26 You choose the place on the mountain that fits you and feels like home to your soul. Just remember that no

matter how it looks from the valley there is *plenty* of room at the top.

Chapter 26

Let it roll off, like water on a duck's back.

1 If you've lived more than ten years then you probably know that everybody has something to say. Not all of it deserves a home in your spirit.

2 Those who criticize, complain, and agitate often stir the pot just to see who jumps.

3 If you're not careful, their words can seep into your soul like cold rain through a thin coat. That's why I tell folks to learn how to let fruitless reproach, blame, or condemnation roll off you like water rolls off a duck's back.

4 Watch a duck long enough and you'll see something holy. Rain falls. Ripples splash. The duck glides on, unbothered, unsoaked, untouched at the core. The water doesn't penetrate because that bird was designed with a God-given, built-in oil that keeps the storm from sinking it. The storm may touch the surface, but it cannot drown the soul.

5 That's what emotional and spiritual maturity looks like.

6 You cannot live a good life, a purposeful life, or a life without regret if every insult, every rumor, every misunderstanding, every sideways comment, and every bit of nonsense clings to you.

7 Some people wear offense like a wet coat, letting it weigh them down for years. They replay the wound, rehearse the negativity, and baptize their future in yesterday's foolishness. And then they wonder why joy feels heavy and hope feels far and rest feels special.

8 But the problem is not the storm nor the rain. It's the lack of waterproofing.

9 Letting things roll off doesn't mean you ignore responsibility or avoid accountability. It doesn't mean you become numb or unreachable.

10 Letting things roll off means you've grown wise enough to discern what merits your energy and what deserves release.

11 Some criticisms need to be considered. Some corrections need to be received. But some comments need to be dismissed the moment they hit your skin.

12 A duck doesn't argue with the rain. And you don't need to argue with every opinion.

13 Half the things thrown at you are reflections of someone else's fear, insecurity, or confusion rather than a prophecy about your identity. Holding onto them is like carrying someone else's luggage uphill while wondering why your own journey feels so heavy.

14 To let words roll off requires three things: clarity, confidence, and consecration.

15 Clarity reminds you who you are—and whose you are—so you don't internalize every stray thought tossed your way. They may come, but don't let them land. Don't give them a home within you.

16 Confidence keeps you rooted in your worth, so you can withstand the momentary splash of someone else's judgment.

17 Consecration keeps your spirit connected to God through prayer, stillness, and truth so even big storms can't soak you.

18 Know that people will test your waterproofing. Some intentionally, some unknowingly. They will say something slick under their breath. They will misjudge you. They will try to pull you into battles that don't belong to you. But you cannot afford to pick up every offense.

19 A person who grabs every stone thrown at them never has free hands to build anything meaningful.

20 Building towards meaning is how you let the shallow things stay shallow.

21 Growing and maturing is how you stop bending to every breeze.

22 It is important because life is too short, purpose is too precious, and peace is too expensive to let others' opinions stick to you.

23 So let the rain come, let the words fly, let the noise rise, then let it all roll off, just like water on a duck's back.

Chapter 27

After you have done all you can, shake the dust from your feet and move on.

1 There will come a time in your life when your effort with folks or organizations reaches the end of its road.

2 Yes, you poured out your best with sincerity and intention. You tried everything you knew to do. Prayed, planned, reasoned, held on, tried again, apologized, adjusted, forgave, stretched, sacrificed, and still the situation just won't shift. The door won't open. The person won't change. The season won't revive. The path will not smooth itself out.

3 That moment is telling you one thing: you have done all you can and are standing at the place of completion.

4 That leg of your journey is over. You finished what you started. There is no more for you to do in that situation and it's time to shake the dust from your feet and move on.

5 It reminds me of a woman who came to me one day, tired and frustrated about the backsliding on her head chef job at a community college. On day one, she had gone in and reorganized the kitchen and tools, adapted processes for excellent service, and taught her staff everything she knew about maintaining cleanliness. But every morning or so, she returned to work with a smile only to find the kitchen in a mess with staff arguing over whose job it was to keep it clean and in order. Nothing had changed. In her mind, it was worse than when she got there because the workers now knew better.

6 "Have I not given my all?" she asked in an exhale.

7 "Some places," I said, "are meant to teach you, not to keep you. They are assignments for a season and not a sentence for a lifetime."

8 The next morning, she resigned, brought the kitchen to order one last time, and walked out lighter than she had felt in years.

9 When you give your all to no good outcome, it is easier and necessary to shake the dust from your feet and move on.

10 "Dust" is what remains of that effort, emotion, attachment, and expectation. It's the added weight of disappointment from what didn't turn out the way you'd hoped and of pride that wants you to keep trying.

11 If you don't shake that dust off, it follows you and will often cloud your vision, disturb your spirit, and convince you that you should have done more, when in fact you've already given enough.

12 Shaking the dust, then, is a spiritual act of fearless self-respect.

13 It is the release valve for you to not move on in bitterness, anger, or defeat.

14 It is a declaration that your worth is not tied to outcomes and that you know when to cut your losses.

15 It's an acknowledgment that peace is more valuable than staying persistence in the wrong place.

16 And once you shake the dust, you create room for your next blessing.

17 That is in the moving on, admitting that the chapter is closed and what you once believed in no longer exists.

18 Moving on doesn't mean dishonoring what was. It means you are done trying to resurrect something God has already called done.

19 It means you can walk into new strength without carrying old struggles. You can step into new wisdom with old wounds healed. You can go into your next assignment without asking the past for permission.

20 So after you have done all you can, take a deep breath. Bless the road you've traveled. Honor the lessons learned. Feel the heaviness leave your shoulders. And then, with confidence, courage, and quiet authority shake the dust from your feet and move on.

Chapter 28

To go up, go down.

1 Many people I come across these days, particularly those with important titles, fine clothes, fancy cars, big houses, or large bank accounts, hold a narrow idea about humility.

2 They see the act of being humble as someone who is lowly, weak, and in retreat, certainly the opposite of their desire to be seen, chosen, elevated, and applauded publicly for all to see.

3 Being humble is not that, but rather is rooted in worth and alignment with God.

4 Humility is the rising you begin in private not on stages, pulpits, or in the glow of other people's approval. It is the inward decision to put ego and pride aside and let humility do its sacred work.

5 "To go up, go down" sounds backward until you've lived enough life to know that it is only the first step in moving forward.

6 I know for myself that it is the powerhouse for upward mobility. How so? Because it grounds you in ways that keep your character from drifting higher than your wisdom can sustain.

7 When you choose humility, you are choosing God's way of strength, not man's way.

8 When you humble yourself, it is a signal to God that you are willing to listen and open to be taught.

9 It says that you are confident enough in who you are to descend into building depth before height, roots before branches, substance before spotlight, and foundation before the house.

10 In the descent, active stillness takes place much like a seed before it blooms.

11 The excavator of self-examination turns on and begins to clear ascension blockages, such as

comparison, pride, entitlement, self-importance, and the need to be right, revered, or recognized.

12 A sturdier foundation of you forms, one that can handle your amplified integrity, empathy, discernment, and spiritual clarity.

13 And not just for you. Rising through humility carries a gravity that pulls others upward too. Your elevation benefits more than yourself.

14 People trust you faster. They lean in more willingly. They listen more deeply. Why? Because humility makes room for others, and in making room for others, you create space for genuine influence.

15 That's how it was with me when I became moderator of the Northwestern Baptist Association Number One, overseeing and leading more than twenty-five churches across seven counties. I went in to serve, focused only on growing our association, strengthening its member churches, and giving back to our communities rather than making a name for myself. And that's what I did for nearly thirty years, leaving the organization in great shape.

16 The ascent of most admired figures is never built solely on talent, charisma, or brilliance. It is built on the quiet, unseen decisions to kneel before climbing, to learn before leading, to serve before speaking, and to surrender before soaring.

17 When you feel life calling you higher, don't resist the descent.

18 Go down into humility, into truth, into discipline, into the work no one praises so you may rise.

Chapter 29

Get a good understanding.

1 The biblical book of Proverbs—a great treasury of wisdom, often credited to the wise King Solomon—repeatedly urges us to pursue understanding as one of life's highest callings.

2 Again and again, Scripture presses the point: "With all thy getting, get understanding" (Proverbs 4:7).

3 It blesses the seeker, declaring, "Happy is the man that findeth wisdom, and the man that getteth understanding" (Proverbs 3:13).

4 And still, the charge is repeated with urgency: "Get wisdom, get understanding" (Proverbs 4:5).

5 Then, Amos 3:3 backs that up, asking this simple yet thoughtful question: "Can two walk together, except they be agreed?" They cannot. And of course, there is no agreement without understanding.

6 Heaven is not subtle on this matter—understanding is not optional. It is essential to living well and without regret.

7 Life itself echoes this same call for understanding.

8 We feel its absence in the sharp sting of an argument with a spouse or close friend that could have been avoided with better listening.

9 We see it in the breakdown of machinery that a careful reading of the instructions would have prevented.

10 Again and again, experience joins Scripture in testifying: much heartache is not caused by fate, but by a failure to understand.

11 If truth be told—and I'm about to tell it—each of us is far better off with understanding than without it.

12 Getting a good understanding is the difference between motion and true progress, between noise and meaning, between reaction and wisdom.

13 It's like a treasure that rewards you with clarity before you conclude and act on a matter. It is like a guard that protects you from manipulation, poor judgment, wasted time, and misguided choices. It is like a compass that helps you change course when you realize you are headed the wrong way.

14 In your work and on your job, understanding makes you reliable and effective. From a spiritual perspective, it opens you to revelation and alignment. In decision-making, it helps you see consequences before they arrive.

15 So why, then, are we sometimes reluctant to get understanding?

16 Why does it seem that so few pursue it? Because understanding is neither automatic nor passive. It is intentional. It requires effort—enough to ask questions, seek clarity, listen deeply, and return to a truth again and again until its meaning settles into your bones.

17 Too many people live by assumptions, half-heard truths, and surface-level interpretations, then wonder why their lives feel chaotic or confused.

18 To get a good understanding, you must first want it.

19 Then you must slow down and allow your mind to sit with what is being said instead of sprinting past it.

When you rush to give quick answers or fast reactions, you mishear. When you skip ahead to your next reply, you misstep.

20 Whenever I fail to clearly understand someone—and I am humble enough to admit when I do—I am quick to ask, "Now, say that again, please." Why? Because I want to hear not only the words, but the heart behind them.

21 Another enemy of understanding is assumption. The moment you assume, you step out of truth and into distortion.

22 Understanding also requires presence, attention, and courage—because it may challenge what you thought you knew, reveal that you were wrong, or call you into growth you did not plan for.

23 Getting a good understanding is an act of humility. It is admitting, "I don't know enough yet." You cannot grow and pretend to know at the same time. One will always cancel the other.

24 With understanding in hand, you can apply it to your spirit, vision, relationships, health, and wealth.

25 For all these reasons, I urge you: in all your getting, get a good understanding.

The Book of BURNETT

Chapter 30

Don't play yourself cheap.

1 The world we live in is full of wolf-hearted people, eager to feast on your self-respect and shove you out of alignment with God—*if you let them.*

2 Even people who greet you as friend will sometimes try to pull you below your own standard, treating your loyalty like an all-you-can-eat buffet—*if you let them.*

3 Whether or not they succeed depends on how you value yourself.

4 What you think about yourself, recognizing your own worth, is vitality important to how well you live your life.

5 Biblical Romans talks about not thinking of yourself more highly than you ought. It doesn't say to *not* think highly of yourself, because if you don't, who will? It means to not see yourself as better than anyone else.

6 Too many wholesome, brilliant, God-touched people reduce their worth to low levels based on what others think. They stand there as if they were lucky to be invited to the table, when in truth, they brought the value to it.

7 I've watched men and women discount their own gifts and talents while begging for validation from folks who weren't qualified to judge them in the first place.

8 I've known that situation and learned very quickly that it is playing yourself cheap or selling yourself short.

9 It's a slow downfall. You start by underpricing your talent, then you undervalue your voice, then you underestimate your purpose. Before long, you're living on sale, marking your own self down before anyone even gets the chance to do it.

10 But here's the problem with that: God never made a bargain-bin human.

11 No, it is us who bargain-bins our own selves.

12 When my wife, our three young children, and I were driving from Georgia to Michigan one summer, we pulled into a small Kentucky town for gas and a quick stretch. The day was hot and we were thirsty for a cold drink, so I asked the worn, slack-jawed gas attendant if there was any ice I could buy for our cooler.

13 He jerked his chin toward a large ice machine sitting just past the pavement. I carried the cooler over, stepping around chunks of ice scattered on the dirt. When I reached the machine, I saw that the door was locked.

14 "Sir, it's locked," I called back to him.

15 Without looking up, he woofed, "Get it there," jabbing his finger down. "Off the ground."

16 Right then, the truth became sharp and obvious. He wasn't offering service; he was extending humiliation.

17 I turned, walked back to my family without ice, and slid into the front seat. My wife, all wide-eyed, saw the answer in my face before I spoke a word. I put the car in gear and drove off.

18 My dignity was not up for sale. And my children would never see their father bend low to someone else's small-minded cruelty that wasn't worth my presence, anger, or words.

19 Remember who you are; not who they tell you to be, and not the narrow view of you they make room for.

20 Hold to that one always. Among others, and when you're alone with no one watching. When making decisions about your health, the company you keep, and what you do with your money. Why? Because you set the thermostat for who you are and how people treat you.

21 And the world will rise to meet the value you put on yourself.

22 Set it high. Set it true. And never under any circumstance play yourself cheap.

Chapter 31

Love is like a rubber ball; it ought to bounce both ways.

1 Love is a powerful force that is not so easily explained or pinned down.

2 More than an emotion, I know love to be a holy energy that covers a multitude of faults instead of condemning them.

3 It is a bond that stitches hearts together in ways only Heaven can say.

4 It is an expression strong enough to step away from conflict, mistreatment, or anything that bruises the

spirit without bitterness taking root, and gentle enough to stay by the bedside of an elder, holding her hand as she takes her last breath.

5 But when you're ignorant to even the slightest depth of love, you may think of it as a one-way street. You give it out but don't look for it back. Or you're glad to receive it but never return it.

6 Yet, love is an active participant in the Universal law of sowing and reaping. It was never meant to be a one-way offering.

7 Shared through various types of relationships, such as with self, God, family, spouse, friends, or acquaintances, it becomes a living exchange. Not a demand. Not a debt. Not a chore.

8 As such, love that you put out ought to return to you, and often more than what you gave.

9 And it comes back carrying something of equal weight: respect, kindness, honesty, consideration, effort, patience, and such. Maybe not in the same form, but in the same spirit.

10 A rubber ball doesn't bounce because you throw it well, it bounces because it's built that way. Love is the same. It naturally finds its way back to you. Not because you begged for it, but because it recognizes where it came from.

11 You, too, will know love by how it behaves. People who say they love you will show it. Maybe not perfectly, but consistently. They will check on you, pour into you, pray with you, laugh with you, stand up for you. As you do the same for them. Both parties giving and receiving.

12 Now, let me tell you something I learned early on: if love doesn't bounce back or when love stops bouncing, then that is your signal to pause and think. It's a revelation of the other person's capacity. It is God whispering, "Son, daughter—stop throwing yourself at places that can't hold you."

13 It's possible that it was never love to begin with. Instead, it may be performance or fear pretending to be love.

14 I've come to know that the sacred bounce of love is one of the surest signs of God's nature within us. Love moves. It responds. It meets you halfway. It remembers your needs, hears your concerns, and honors your presence.

15 Love always bounces back.

Chapter 32

You must know more about a person than just their name.

1 A name tells you almost nothing about a person.

2 A name is identification and an introduction.

3 And if you judge a person by nothing more than what he's called, you might as well judge a car by its shine. You will fool yourself every time.

4 There's nothing wrong with a good name—one with some weight. But a name doesn't make the man; the man makes the name.

5 In every circle you move and especially where you want to make progress—family, work, church, friends,

or anything beyond a polite "hello"—it serves you to learn who people truly are and not just their name.

6 When I was a young man trying to make my way in the world, I used to get impressed when someone walked into the room with a title or a reputation I'd heard whispered about. But I learned quickly that reputation is advertising and character is the product. One can be bought, borrowed, or embellished. The other can only be lived.

7 So now when you meet a person, do like me, and listen past the name, the reputation, and even the packaging.

8 Watch quietly for and pay attention to their character. It will reveal the truth of itself no matter how pretty it's covered up.

9 What fruit does their life bear? How does he treat people who can't give him anything back? How does she handle disappointment, success, and temptation? What does his friend group look like?

10 What are her values, not just her vocabulary? How do those values show themselves?

11 Some folks can talk kindness but can't live it. Some folks will praise God on Sunday morning and curse you on Monday afternoon. Some will tell you they love you with their mouths while betraying you with their

habits. "Lord, Lord" means nothing without the life to match.

12 You can learn more about a person in ten minutes of observation than in ten years of titles.

13 Trust patterns, not promises. Integrity, not impression. They will inform your decisions and let you know how best to relate, if at all, with what you see.

14 Don't hire someone because you like their name. Don't date someone because their name sounds good attached to yours. Don't put faith in someone's name when their actions have yet to show up.

15 A name is easy to learn. It tells you *who* not *what* a person is. But learning a person—what she stands for, whether he can walk with you in truth and honor—takes time and intelligence.

16 Let knowing more about a person than just their name be your secret sauce to walking wisely through this world.

Chapter 33

When it comes to money, save some and spend some.

1 I know what it's like to walk down the street with not one cent in my pocket—hungry, humbled, and praying nobody asked me for anything.

2 And I know what it's like to stroll that same street years later with my pockets full—grateful, grounded, and remembering every step it took to get from empty to overflow.

3 The tough, worrisome, and prayerful times between those two pockets—one empty, one full—drove home to me the truth that money is a servant you manage, not a master you obey. It is a tool you steward, not a god you serve. It is an instrument you draw, not an aim you chase. It is a test that reveals who you are just as quickly as it provides what you need.

4 Somewhere in the middle of lack and abundance, wisdom whispered, *"Hold some. Use some. And don't let either extreme own you."*

5 Don't let money own you.

6 This taught me to regard every dollar and learn how to handle it with gratitude and good sense, spending with purpose and saving with vision.

7 Save some and spend some. Not either-or. Both. Because either edge—spending everything or saving everything— will leave you wobbling like a fool on an economic cliff.

8 If you spend every dollar the moment it touches your hand, you'll stay working twice as hard for half as much peace.

9 And if you clutch every penny so tightly that copper stains your fingers, you'll live a small, pitiful life, mistaking hoarding for wisdom.

10 Money is currency. It is meant to flow, not recklessly and not fearfully but responsibly. Generously. Intentionally.

11 Spend some on what matters, like the roof over your head, the people you love, the memories that feed your spirit, and the tools that help you grow.

12 The Christmas season was always a time of joy, love, and laughter in our home. Each year, I would ask my young children to name the one special thing they hoped to receive. Their wishes were often big—an Easy-Bake oven, a minibike, a BB gun, and the like—no small requests for a family on a tight budget. Still, those desires mattered to my wife and me. We believed that wonder and hope were as essential to a child as food and shelter, and so we searched for wise, creative ways to honor their hearts without breaking our means.

13 This is an example of how to let your money reflect your values rather than satisfy your hasty impulses or bury your insecurities.

14 But save some, too. Save for the days you pray never come. Save for the dreams that need time and resources to bring to life. Save for the opportunities God sends your way that only preparedness can grab. Saving is about being wise and steady, not about being scared.

15 Spend some. Save some. That simple rhythm has carried generations before you. It will carry you too—if you let it. So let it.

Chapter 34

Starting well is good—nothing wrong with that—but it's how you finish that counts.

1 I met a lot of people who came out of the gate looking like champions. Strong start. Bright shine. Good stride. Plenty of applause from the crowd.

2 Some folks know how to make an entrance, wearing a clean suit, bright smile, and polished talk. And there's nothing wrong with that.

3 Starting well is good as long as it's true. It sets the tone. It shows intention. It tells the world you're serious.

4 But what I know from watching people rise and sometimes fall, it's not the start that determines your destiny. It's the finish.

5 Life will teach you quickly that early shine can fade, early strength can tire, and early applause can quiet down to silence when the real race sets in.

6 Some people who started their careers with promise couldn't finish because their discipline didn't match their dreams. Some marriages that began like fairy tales failed because the couple's vows and dance didn't keep pace with change. Plenty of people who talk big talk in January skip out on the walk by March.

7 Most anybody can sprint the first hundred yards. It's finishing the whole race through heat, hills, doubts, and detours that reveals the depth of the person you are becoming.

8 Finishing requires something deeper than enthusiasm. It requires stamina of spirit. It requires a commitment that holds even when the path gets narrow and the crowd gets thin.

9 Starting uses adrenaline. Finishing uses character.

10 Character is built in the middle miles where nobody's cheering, when progress is slow, when you're not even sure if you're still moving forward. That's where your heart is trained. That's where your faith is forged. That's where the finish line is quietly decided.

11 When I started preaching, I didn't start with a big church or a national stage. I was called to pastor a small congregation of people with big hearts and genuine love for God. People who chose hope over perfection. They worshiped in a cramped wooden building that looked like a strong wind could lay it flat.

12 I finished strong, growing my congregation and other churches, because I kept showing up and not quitting when the shine and the applause wore off.

13 I finished focused because I didn't confuse momentum with mission, choosing integrity over popularity and staying steady even when my knees shook.

14 I finished without regret because every day I lived the sermons that I preached rather than just deliver them, keeping my eyes on the finish line.

15 And that finish line doesn't grade your stumbles, pauses, or missteps onto the long road or the wrong road. It honors your endurance to the end.

16 So yes, start well if you can. Nothing wrong with that. If you start with the end in mind. If you start to finish, whatever that may look like.

17 Life is not handing out trophies for the best first mile. It's how you finish that counts. And you still have time to finish strong.

Chapter 35

Count the cost to build the house before you start to build.

1 According to Proverbs 29:18, having vision and purpose is key to life moving forward spiritually and personally.

2 Turning vision into reality, I learned, requires discipline, devotion, and steady, often simple work.

3 But before you act on the vision to build the "house", which could be for you a business, a marriage, a ministry, a career, or a new version of yourself, you must first count the cost. Not to discourage the dream, but to strengthen the dreamer.

4 Counting the cost is spiritual arithmetic.

5 It causes you to ask yourself, "Do I have the character to sustain what I'm asking for? Do I have the patience to build slowly? Do I have the humility to learn? Do I have the courage to continue when inspiration fades and commitment must take over?"

6 You see, some folks try to build gallon-sized dreams upon cup-sized foundations.

7 They start framing walls before checking their footing. They decorate before stabilizing. They get swept up in excitement and skip the excavation—the quiet, internal clearing that ensures what they build doesn't crumble under pressure.

8 When you count the cost, you honor the vision by preparing for it.

9 You gather the right tools. You strengthen the weak places. You set boundaries. You calculate what must be invested, what must be sacrificed, and what must be protected at all costs.

10 If the truth be told—and I'm about to tell it—anything worth building requires a desire coupled with readiness.

11 Counting the cost to build the house before you start to build will reward you with wisdom to build with

intention something that will stand, or to not build at all.

Chapter 36

Take chances, yes, but calculated chances.

1 Moving forward always asks something of you. A leap here. A bold step there.

2 I learned that lesson more than once. When I bought land on the road that I grew up on to build a house. When I opened a laundromat in the "projects" exactly where and when it was needed. When I accepted the position of moderator to lead an association of more than twenty-five churches. And so on.

3 I saw none of these actions as gambling or thrill-seeking. That wasn't me.

4 They were calculated moves. I did the homework to know which ones matched me so that I didn't chase everything. And each one offered rise or expansion, even the ones that were short-lived. They were Spirit-brought opportunities, taken with courage and as much clear thinking as possible.

5 My daughter had been on her corporate marketing job about seven years when she sat down with me in my den, seeking council. She wanted to leave her job to start a Christian magazine business.

6 I knew nothing about that business, but I knew to ask my five key questions to gauge her level of calculation in leaping from employee to entrepreneur with both feet and a steady heart.

7 What real problem are you solving and for whom?

8 How long can you hold up yourself financially while the carrying and growing the business—what does the math look like?

9 What is your clear plan for finding, attracting, getting, and keeping subscribers and advertisers?

10 What makes you the best person to build this, now?

11 What is God saying to you about both the reward if this works and the lesson if it doesn't?

12 "You're young," I started, after she satisfied my inquiry. "Nothing beats a failure but a try. Give it a shot. Do your best. You can always get a job later if need be."

13 She founded and ran *Say Amen* Magazine for five years, selling its assets at a profit when she found out that she was pregnant with my fifth grandson.

14 Calculated chances are where faith and wisdom shake hands.

15 It's easy to see risky steps as right. They tend to be shiny and grand and promise a fast track to riches.

16 But at the root of most spoiled dreams is loose, unquestioned courage; bravery without a blueprint; hope that hasn't done its homework; motion with no meaning.

17 A leap without calculation is just a fall with optimism.

18 But a calculated chance is a step onto a path you've studied, prayed over, prepared for, and strengthened yourself to walk.

19 Your fear may still whisper its warnings, but your wisdom speaks louder.

20 And no, calculated chances don't protect you from failure.

21 They prepare you for it by keeping you from being careless with your calling.

22 They help you discern when the door is open and when the door is bait.

23 They turn your life into a series of intentional moves instead of accidental outcomes.

24 While every breakthrough and revelation in your life will require you to put something on the line—say, comfort, reputation, or the illusion of control— calculated chances ensure that what you risk is an investment rather than a sacrifice.

25 Take chances, yes. A life without regret demands it.

26 But take the kind that stretch you without snapping you, the kind that build you without breaking you, the kind where you move boldly, but not blindly.

Chapter 37

Charity begins at home and spreads abroad.

1 When I used to hear as a young boy the old folks say, "Chile, charity begins at home and then spreads abroad," I thought they were talking about giving money.

2 Money may have been part of it, but not nearly all of it.

3 Life showed me that they meant something far deeper.

4 A lot of folks want to be known as generous, patient, or wise to the wider world, but they're short-tempered, selfish, or careless at home. They give the community their best and give their family their leftovers. And that's not charity. That's imbalance. That's ego wearing a halo.

5 If your goodness only works in public, it's not goodness. It's a bid for attention and acceptance.

6 Charity is monetary generosity, yes. But it is also the discipline of treating the people closest to you— starting with yourself—with the same kindness, respect, patience, and accountability you're quick to give strangers.

7 The real test of charity begins within—where you learn to offer love to your own self along with its companions of truth, mercy, correction, compassion, and joy. When you honor your own soul first, generosity flows outward with ease, not strain.

8 From self, you spread charity to those behind your own front door. With how you honor the people you live with, share your table with, and walk with.

9 How do you speak to your spouse? How do you handle your children when you're tired, frustrated, or disappointed? How do you treat the people who know your moods, flaws, habits, and history?

10 Only after igniting at home in private can charity spread naturally in public. The grace you extend to those closest to you matures into the kind of kindness you offer—wisely, respectfully, and appropriately—to neighbors, coworkers, and even the strangers life places in your path.

11 When you genuinely treat people well at home, you become the kind of person who treats people well everywhere. Your house becomes a training ground for your humanity. Your family becomes the first classroom where you learn and teach compassion, forgiveness, humility, patience, accountability, and love.

12 If you can look your spouse in the eye after failing him or her and say, "I'm sorry," then you can apologize anywhere.

13 If you can listen to your child's fears without dismissing him or her, then you can listen to a stranger's pain without judgment.

14 If you can serve the people under your own roof, you can serve others without pride.

15 Charity starts like a seed planted in familiar soil and then grows outward. So, start the work at home, then spread it abroad.

16 That's how a life becomes a blessing. That's how a family becomes a legacy. That's how a person becomes whole.

Chapter 38

Don't give 'em a stick to crack your head with.

1 One of the sharpest pieces of advice ever handed to me came wrapped in a warning: "Don't give 'em a stick to crack your head with."

2 Often in life, folk will come after you for this reason or the other. Not everyone. It may be coworkers nervous about your progress. Sometimes they're friends who feel more comfortable when things are stirred up than when they are quiet. Or they're relatives who remember the old you and want that person back.

3 For them to manufacture something out of nothing is one thing. There's very little, if anything, you can do about that.

4 What you can do, though, is your best not to hand them a reason to knock you down, put your business in the street, or derail your life.

5 The sticks people may use against you are often the ones you dropped.

6 A missed deadline. A careless comment. A bad decision you made in a hurry. A secret you should have kept between you and God. A weakness you refused to address until it became a headline.

7 Not giving them a stick is about using wisdom to live mindful, measured, and mature in alignment with who you say you are and where you intend to go.

8 This is about you, not them. About intention, not paranoia.

9 When you live willfully, you stop volunteering for trouble. You stop leaving your integrity unattended. You stop letting your emotions run errands your character doesn't want to pay for. You start realizing that people cannot use against you what you never give them.

10 This is especially important in a world where folks love a lie and a scandal more than a solution. One mistake can go farther than a hundred good deeds. Some people will watch your life like a fine timepiece, not to learn from you but to find the speck of sawdust they can blow up in your face. And if you're not careful, you'll turn on their blower while expecting mercy.

11 The good news is that you get to choose and dictate most of what happens in your life.

12 You get to choose where you share your heart or when to be silent, knowing that everybody can't be trusted with your vulnerabilities nor your dreams.

13 You get to choose who sees your unpolished places, knowing that everybody can't be trusted with your past.

14 You control your reactions. You control your decisions. You control your boundaries. You control what you reveal, how you show up, and where you stand.

15 Stand on the side of truth, Godliness, and you.

16 This doesn't mean live stiff, scared, or suspicious. It means live aware. Aware that your future is too precious to sabotage. Aware that your reputation is too

valuable to cheapen. Aware that your spirit is too expensive to let just anyone handle.

17 It means living in such a way that if someone comes for you, they come empty-handed.

18 It means living with such integrity that even lies can't stick.

19 It means living with character so deep that any stone thrown bounces off righteousness.

20 Because a wise person doesn't walk around fearing what others might do. A wise person simply refuses to hand out sticks.

Chapter 39

Finish what you start.

1 One of my top truths for living without regret is that while starting well is good, it's how you finish that counts (read more about that in Chapter 34). This truth adds that it's not only *how* you finish but *that* you finish.

2 Starting can be easy. We all know the rush of a new idea, the thrill of fresh beginnings, the excitement of stepping into promise with puff in your chest and plans in your pocket.

3 Think about newlyweds, running out of a church to showers of rice. Business partners at the ribbon cutting

ceremony of their new office. Or college graduates tossing their caps into the air.

4 Beginnings arrive dressed in hope, begging to be announced and celebrated.

5 But life doesn't hinge on what you *start*. It is built on what you *finish*.

6 A half-built house leaks. A half-written book offers half a story. A half-lived promise breaks somebody's heart.

7 There is no need to lay a foundation for something you won't have the courage to finish. This goes for buildings as well as relationships, dreams, disciplines, and faith.

8 Luke 14:28-30 put it this way: "For which of you, intending to build a tower, sit not down first, and count the cost, whether he have sufficient to finish it? Lest haply, after he hath laid the foundation, and is not able to finish it, all that behold it begin to mock him, saying, This man began to build, and was not able to finish."

9 Too many people collect beginnings like souvenirs and leave a trail of unfinished business behind them.

10 Tough times is a signal for them to quit. They see inconvenience as an invitation to sit down. When it stops feeling good, they call it growth and walk away.

11 There will always be reasons not to finish. You'll get tired. You'll get busy. You'll get distracted. You'll get discouraged. Something shinier will come along. Something easier will call your name. That's not a sign to stop. It's a test to see whether you are building your life on feeling or commitment.

12 Finishing doesn't mean foolish grit, though. Wisdom knows when a season has ended. But most people don't quit because the season is done.

13 They quit because the work got real. Why? Because real requires endurance, patience, and a decision that outlives your moods.

14 You don't find out who you are when everything is new. You find out who you are when it's old, heavy, slow, and silent. And you keep showing up anyway.

15 I learned over the years that finishing does something starting never can.

16 Finishing builds character.

17 Anybody can be inspired on day one. It takes integrity to show up on day nine hundred.

18 Anybody can make a promise in a high moment, swept up in excitement, enthusiasm, or emotion. It takes maturity, discipline, and character to keep that promise when the feeling fades, when obstacles

appear, or when life becomes inconvenient. True integrity is proven not in the moment of pledge, but in the steadfast follow-through.

19 When you finish what you start, even if you must adjust (and you will), you teach your soul that your word is truth and reliable. You train your spirit not to wince at resistance. You tell Heaven you can go the distance, you can see things through.

20 What I do know is that God blesses faithfulness. And faithfulness is proven in the follow-through.

21 Some of the strongest and most successful people I know refused to abandon their goal mid-air. They kept hammering when the wood got hard. They kept praying when the answers were slow. They kept believing when the evidence was thin. And one day, they looked up and realized the thing they almost quit was the very blessing waiting on the other side of tough, hiding behind inconvenience, and waiting beyond the weariness.

22 So, if you start it, then finish it. The same way biblical Paul finished his race, finish your education. Finish the healing you started. Finish the work God put on your hands. Finish becoming who you said you wanted to be.

23 Because the crown is not for the fastest beginner. The crown is for the faithful finisher.

The Book of BURNETT

Chapter 40

Everything to know isn't in a book.

1 Books are sacred companions. They carry the breadth of experience across generations, preserving what others learned the hard way so we might learn it sooner.

2 I was blessed to have many books in my home library. I relied on them, trusted them, studied them, and leaned on them over and over again for information and insight to help guide my ministry.

3 Still, one truth has proven itself again and again: everything worth knowing cannot be found on a page.

4 Some lessons only arrive through living—and through the quiet inner revelations of God, the Infinite Intelligence that no book can fully contain.

5 You can read about fire, yet only heat will teach you how quickly it burns.

6 You can read about love, but only heartbreak teaches you its cost and its depth.

7 You can read about faith, but only disaster reveals whether you truly have it.

8 Books can inform the mind, but life is the instructor of the soul.

9 There are truths no classroom can deliver. The way silence sounds when loss walks into your house. The way courage feels when fear is louder than your hope. The way responsibility weighs when mouths depend on your obedience. These are not footnotes. These are revelations.

10 I learned early that wisdom shows up in overalls just as often as it does in suited-up lecture halls. I learned it from laboring hands, from wrinkled faces, from quiet men who spoke few words but lived honest lives. I learned it from my wife's steady faith when the bills were taller than our paychecks. I learned it from my children when they watched not what I preached, but what I practiced.

11 And some of the deepest knowledge I carry never came from a book. It came from a mistake.

12 Failure taught me what pride would not. Waiting taught me what haste never could. Loss taught me what abundance had hidden. Pain has been a brutal teacher, but it has never lied.

13 Experience doesn't quote theory; it writes truth directly onto the heart.

14 That does not lessen the value of books. It completes it.

15 Knowledge read but never lived is only information. Knowledge lived becomes wisdom. A shelf full of books may make you learned, but a life full of careful, calculated steps makes you wise.

16 There are also some things God will not explain in advance. If you knew everything ahead of time, you would never need to walk by faith. The journey would become a schedule instead of a surrender. God teaches some lessons only "on the way." Only after the prayer. Only after the leap. Only after the fall. Only after the healing.

17 You cannot read your way into endurance. You must endure your way into it.

18 You cannot study your way into patience. You must wait your way into it.

19 You cannot research your way into forgiveness. You must bleed your way into that knowing.

20 And yet, how quick we are to look for another book when what we need is courage. How quick we are to seek a new sermon when what we need is obedience. How quick we are to quote wisdom we refuse to practice.

21 Everything to know isn't in a book, but everything in a book is meant to be lived.

22 Understanding grows when knowledge meets experience and obedience becomes habit. The lesson doesn't settle in the mind until it has passed through the hands. Truth does its greatest work only when it is practiced under pressure.

23 Wisdom is found in the living room, not just the library. It is learned in strained relationships, in quiet integrity, in keeping one's word when breaking it would be easier. It is shaped in decision-making, in delayed gratification, in choosing peace over pride, and truth over comfort.

24 So read. Study. Learn. But do not stop there.

25 Let your life become the final chapter. Let your choices be the footnotes. Let your obedience be the commentary. And when the book runs out, trust that God is still teaching—through circumstance, through consequence, through grace.

26 Because some truths are too heavy for paper. They must be carried by the living.

Chapter 41

Trust in the one true God within you.

1 I got saved, baptized, and joined my church at a young age. I learned Bible scriptures and how to pray and serve the living God, and quickly became a church leader.

2 For me, "church" wasn't just a Sunday event. It was everyday living. It was a fire that swelled up from inside me, birthing in me the desire to listen to and walk with God moment by moment.

3 By seventeen, I was teaching Sunday School. Later, I became a deacon, and then superintendent of Sunday School, and then Chairman of the Deacons' Board. At thirty-seven, when the pastor of our church died, I led

the congregation for nine months until we installed a new pastor. At forty, I heard a whisper of a call from God to preach the Gospels, to become a minister.

4 That's when I quieted the voice that I'd followed all this time to make space for questions—and doubt, an act that was strange to me.

5 I hadn't asked for this, had I? Was this where my passion had been leading me? Why me, Lord, why me?

6 My voice isn't for preaching, I thought. I don't sing too well. I don't know how to hoop. Who wants to hear me?

7 For some three months, I wrestled with the call that had merged with that fire burning within me. I told only my wife who comforted me as I tossed and turned in bed. I drove to work and back, debating the ups and downs of "what if". I walked my backyard, testing out my vocals, my moans, and my groans.

8 What I thought of as running from "the call" was really a slow way of saying yes to it. Then my revelation hit: this is not about what *I* can do. It's about what *God* can do. It's about God expressing through me—the way it had been all along.

9 With the fire and that revelation, I announced that I was accepting the call into ministry. It was one of the best decisions of my life.

10 Trusting the God within is trusting the voice that knows the difference between your fears and your future.

11 It is trusting the intuition that nudges you toward growth, the conviction that rises when you're tempted to shrink, the peace that refuses to be bullied by doubt and chaos, and the wisdom that whispers, *"This way, son."*

12 The God within is the compass that never lies, even when your emotions do.

13 It is truth-telling when your doubts run loud.

14 It is the eternal calm beneath your temporary storms.

15 It is the essence of your true self, not the watered-down self you show the world.

16 To trust the God within is to trust that you were made with intention and equipped with instructions.

17 It is to honor that still, small voice that speaks in knowing rather than noise.

18 It is to admit that the same power that hung galaxies, parted seas, and breathes life into every being did not suddenly run out of good sense when it came to making you.

19 Trusting the God that never leaves you requires courage. Why? Because God will call you higher.

20 God will ask you to get rid of the excuses and smallness you keep in your back pocket.

21 God will demand that you honor the call on your life even when you and others don't understand it.

22 The God within will lead you into rooms that your insecurity will say you don't belong in and ask you to forgive when your ego wants revenge.

23 God will pull you toward purpose when fear prefers stagnation and whisper instructions that don't always match what the crowd wants.

24 Will trusting that voice feel risky? Yes. That's exactly what I felt when I heard the whisper to become a preacher.

25 But the greater risk is ignoring it. Running and trying to hide from God fills your life with friction. You feel off-center, out of rhythm, slightly hollow. You chase validation and miss alignment. You make decisions that look smart but feel wrong. You move, but you don't advance.

26 When you trust the true God within, you begin to live from the inside out, not the outside in.

27 Your peace becomes non-negotiable. Your purpose becomes clearer. Your confidence becomes grounded, not performative. Your choices become aligned, not frantic. Your life becomes guided, not guessed at.

28 You walk with divine authority, quiet certainty, and a soul that knows it is *never* alone.

Chapter 42

There's only one way to go, and that's forward.

1 There is no reverse gear in life.

2 No matter how long you sit and stare behind you, nothing is there except memories. The road only runs in one direction.

3 Yesterday is gone. You can remember it. You can learn from it. You can even grieve it. But you cannot live there. You cannot go backwards.

4 There's only one way to go, and that's forward.

5 Some people build whole houses in the past. They furnish it with regret, paint it with guilt, and lock it from the inside with fear. They replay old conversations, old mistakes, old wins, and old losses as though repeating them will somehow rewrite or revive them.

6 They get stuck because they are afraid of failing again. Or they are awaiting an apology that may never come. Or because someone told them that they would never amount to anything and they believed it.

7 The familiar pain starts to feel safer than the unknown promise ahead.

8 But deciding to stay stuck in the past costs more than stepping forward. Often, it costs you your opportunity to build a fulfilling life.

9 The past should serve us as a teacher, not a home. It's meant to be a classroom where we learn what to do or what not to do for the future.

10 Forward is where you demonstrate, step by step, that you learned the lesson and can carry it without dragging its weight.

11 Forward is where you refuse to let the past define who you are. You're able to tell your story without shackling your future to it.

12 Forward is where God meets you and lights up your course *as* you go, sharpening your faith to believe that what's ahead is better than what's behind.

13 The truth is that God is always calling you forward, beckoning you onward rather than chaining you to what was.

14 And in your forward movement, the holy intention is that you are stepping in the right direction—toward who you are and the life you want to live, not back toward what once tried to bind or reduce you.

15 I've learned that you don't need perfect clarity to move forward. Marching in the right direction requires humility to admit that you don't see or know everything.

16 It requires faith and the quiet, daily obedience of taking one more step even when you don't exactly know where you're heading.

17 Why? Because God rarely shows the whole staircase, choosing instead to illuminate the next step and see whether your faith will stand on it.

18 That faith will cause you to get up when you're tired. To apologize even when you're right. To start over when you swore you never would.

19 Determination, maturity, and beginning again are just three examples of forward movement. Or in another word, growth.

20 Forward is where growth knows the importance of keeping closed doors closed, saying bye to relationships that have completed their course, and letting expired dreams go.

21 You won't go forward without resistance.

22 Gravity favors backward. Shame favors backward. Fear favors backward. And people who are comfortable with the old version of you will always pull backward.

23 But the future does not answer to ease. It responds to your courage.

24 And every step forward, no matter how small, rearranges your confidence. You don't just move into new places; you become a new person while moving.

25 Every step forward teaches you how strong you are. It teaches you to shed fear of the unknown, of failure, or of what others think. It teaches you to invite more possibility and what could be. It teaches you to focus, avoiding sideways that only distract you.

26 With God, there's only one way to go—and that's forward, into what the Spirit is still shaping and stirring within you with every faithful step.

The Line That Carries Us

Before there were chapters, there was a life lived out loud in faith, work, laughter, and love. These images highlight the sacred line that carries us forward, and at the center of them all stands our father, Rev. Burnett S. Jackson.

These photographs are more than just images; they are witnesses. They echo the stories you've read, the truths you've encountered, and the wisdom shaped through one man's heart after God and devotion to family and community. His breath became our breath. His courage still pulses in our steps. His faith and fire live on in our bones.

Here you will see just a tad of the man behind the words—the husband, the father, the pastor, the builder, the servant. This is not merely remembrance; this is inheritance made visible.

May these photos deepen the voice you've been hearing all along. May they remind you that a good life leaves footprints long after it leaves the earth—and that the truest legacies are not written only in books, but in bloodlines, in faithful living, and in the souls forever changed along the way.

Rev. B.S. Jackson, Pastor's Anniversary,
July 13, 2014

Rev. B.S. and Zelda Jackson, Pastor's Anniversary,
July 14, 2013

With Zelda, Terry, Faye, and Al on summer vacation
2001

With seven of eight grandchildren, Christmas 2013

The eldest grandson and his prayed-for bride, 2014

Shiloh Baptist Church, Athens, Georgia

Northwestern Baptist Association #1 Moderator business, here with the late Rev. Dr. Cameron Alexander, 1991

With Al and Faye on that trip to Detroit, 1969

Laundromat opening newspaper article, 1970

With Zelda, Terry, and Al in front of the brick house, 1961

Acknowledgments

With deep gratitude, I honor my brothers, Terry and Al, for endorsing this passion project, for helping to keep Dad's voice alive in our hearts and on these pages, and for sticking together as Dad wanted, as he charged us. I appreciate how we can remember Dad and Mom in joy, in laughter, in awe, and in the decisions we make each day.

Special thanks to Gerard Munajj of Graphic Image Design for capturing the soul of this book through a cover that mirrors Dad's worn Bible and whispers of his journey before a single word is read. Gerard's artistry gave this work its first voice and invited readers into a space where Dad's presence is felt immediately.

To my core heart and ride-or-die crew—W.J., Jay, Simcha, and William—thank you for your unwavering support, your thoughtful questions and ideas, your patience, and your love as I stole away into The Sanctuary to write. You held space for the work when the work demanded more of me, never letting me feel alone in the process. Your presence (including the jokes), encouragement, and faith in me and my writing made this creation possible, and I will always be grateful.

To Shiloh Baptist Church—our forever family and my father's faithful child—thank you for loving Rev. Burnett S. Jackson not only as your pastor, but as your own. For nearly fifty years you walked with him in faith, vision, struggle, and triumph. You prayed with him, labored beside him, built with him, and believed with him. You trusted his leadership, endured seasons together, and stood shoulder to shoulder as God unfolded purpose among you. What grew at Shiloh was not just a church, but a living testimony of what happens when love, faith, and commitment meet. You continue to be a shining reflection of God in the community, a warm light for those seeking hope and healing, and a joyful inspiration to me.

And to you, dear reader, thank you for picking up this book and welcoming these truths into your life. May what shaped us bless you, strengthen you, and lift you higher, as Dad's voice continues to speak through every page.